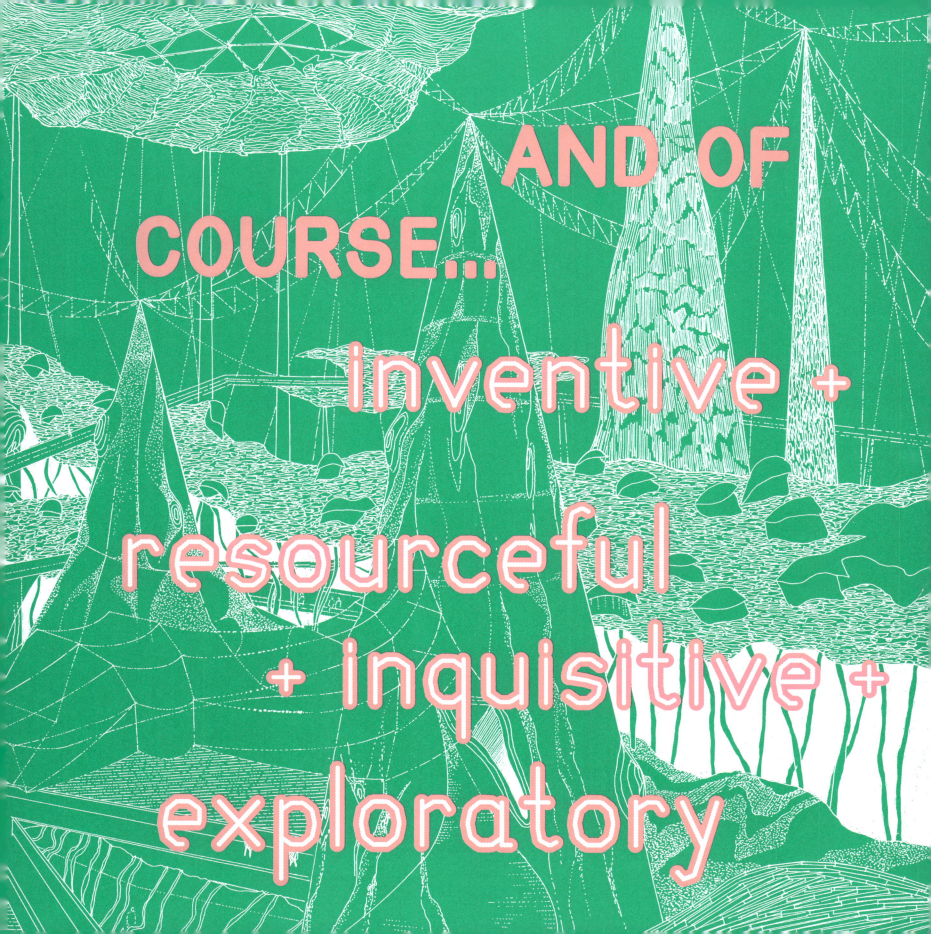

ARCHIGRAM

EDITED BY PETER COOK

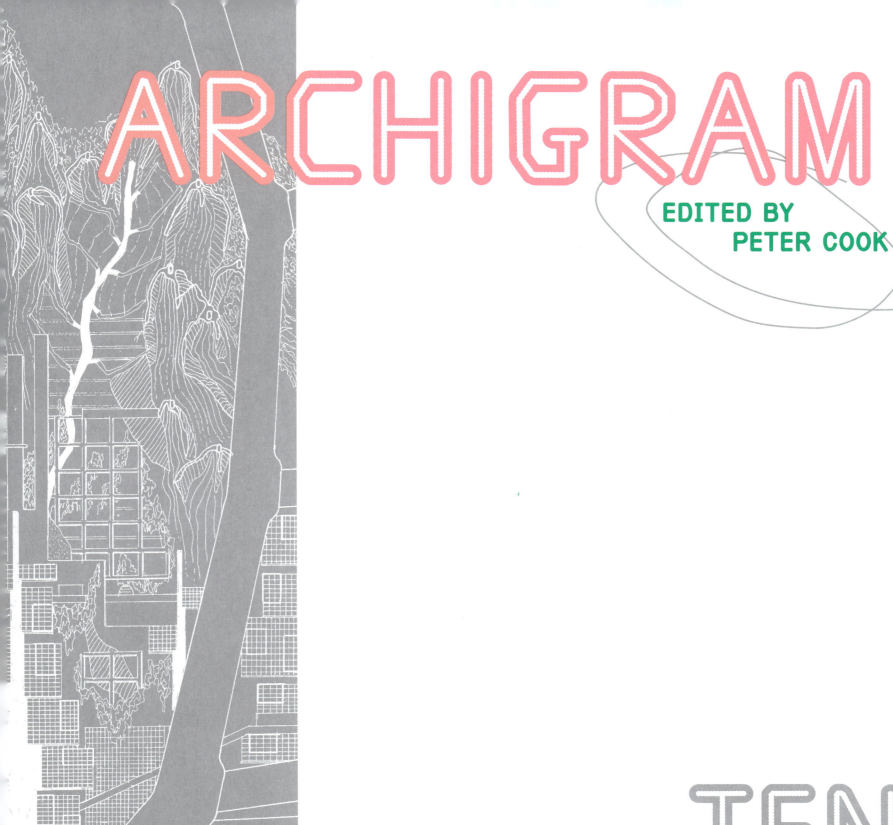

TEN

'So Archigram never went away...?'

AS AN ATTITUDE IT HAS NEVER GONE AWAY
IT IS EVEN MORE NECESSARY THAN EVER
ARCHITECTURE MUST MOVE FORWARD
ARCHITECTURE MUST INVENT

We don't apologise for having ideas and forms, and interweaving dreams with reality. In fact, we embrace strangeness and even inconsistency and even (occasionally) nonsense.

'So what happened in between?'

Po-mo came and went ... and came back again. Deconstructivism liberated some very brilliant people and sent them into the unknown. Then the computer freed them from the predictability of the rectangle. Then came the 'biscuit' architecture of brick / rectangular window / brick / rectangular window / brick / rectangular window ... but peer round the corners, look into strange crevices. Look in the Alps, in Patagonia, in New South Wales, in Guizhou, maybe down the end of your street, and you can find rarely discussed nuggets of built new thinking.

'Archigram continues to show lots of drawings...?'

DRAWINGS ARE EXCITING
DRAWINGS CAN BE WAYWARD
DRAWINGS CAN BE VERY, VERY PRECISE
DRAWINGS CAN BE PRESCIENT

Doodles are a direct, spontaneous link to much of the material that follows.

Yet doodles can often be the unencumbered creative act.

'Maybe Archigram is one collective doodle then...?'

I wouldn't mind that. In fact, I really like that.

Archigram 10 is a great Collective — Creative — Doodle

Perry Kulper

Tomás Saraceno has long sought to make visible the spectral hues, elemental forces, and synaesthetic vectors that shape the web(s) of life, from the terrestrial to the cosmic, from the microscopic to the planetary. Spanning more than two decades, his investigations into utopian urbanisms make sense of the entanglements human and non-human bodies find themselves caught up in, while proposing speculative and realisable models for cohabitation that offer more just, interdependent ways of being together. Across open-source, collective, and interdisciplinary projects, including the Aerocene Foundation (2015–) and Arachnophilia, his work is aimed at rethinking the co-creation of the atmosphere, towards a society free from carbon emissions, for eco-social justice.

Many of the artist's cloud sculptures and expansive installations stem from his long-standing artistic inquiry Cloud Cities, a proposal for a common imaginary for an ethical re-alliance with the environment, the planet, and the cosmic/web of life beyond Anthropocentrism. The cluster-like artworks are composed of a number of interconnected modules constructed with black and reflective panels, forming constellations out of geometric forms inspired by the Weaire–Phelan structure, evocative of aggregating foam or soap bubbles. Some clouds have web-like structures set with them, resonating with the woven habitats of spiders and the cosmic web. This analogy gives rise to imagery of the structure of the observable universe, reminding us that we are all floating on cosmic clouds of galaxies, the perfect major fields of inspiration for Saraceno.

CLOUD CITIES

Tomás Saraceno

Architecture has a responsibility to provide for those things we know will happen, yet we are conscious that so much that is important in our lives happens outside the necessarily reductive reach of the architectural programme. How is it that we can address those instances that we cannot predict and how could we build the knowledge of how to design for conditions of indeterminacy?

The work illustrated here shows some of the drawing instruments constructed to search for ways of thinking about a broader scope of architectural occupation. As they address issues of uncertainty, they operate outside the realms of explicit knowledge. They rehearse possible scenarios to help develop tacit knowledge, learning from didactic instruments of explicit knowledge to develop the means to hold embodied knowledge.

Instruments of Uncertainty

Nat Chard

The first versions relied on optical projection with folding picture planes as critical receivers. The physics of light proved too predictable, so the instruments shifted to projecting latex paint. With optical projection, the image is always captive to the projected figure, but the flying paint (representing an episode of occupation) would splatter against a model to register the nature of the event rather than that of an object. (This version was a collaboration with Perry Kulper).

While working on early versions of these instruments, a fortuitous discovery was made of how to float shadows in mid-air, both in front of your eyes and through stereoscopic photography, enabled by Instrument Six. Given the importance of shadows in establishing the phenomenal presence of architecture and in turn how to represent that presence in drawings through skiagraphy, such a discovery offers an opportunity to disturb the conventions of architecture.

Explicit knowledge is stored and accessed through libraries, archives, and museums. For this project, the equivalent gathering device is a pair of chairs that have parts for storage and display. The aim is to activate the knowledge held in their exhibits as part of daily life. To develop the chair, four versions of Instrument Ten acted out various scenarios using the thrown paint methods developed in Instrument Four onwards.

The three drawings of the chairs appear to be simultaneous but are seen from different views. On closer inspection, there are small discrepancies between them, so that while one might be an accurate record of what took place, the other two might be a recollection or perhaps a perception coloured by the content held by the chairs.

Dora Epstein Jones

YOU CAN'T SAY WE NEVER TRIED

Archigram 10 is out! After an interregnum of let's politely call it, fifty-something years. And so, as with any fifty-something, the hubris of youth can be nostalgically remembered from the safety of one's armchair, comfortably nestled into by a stubborn layer of fat, accompanied by a favourite beverage you once discovered in Rome.

Typically, as you look back at that youth, you envy your own past sexiness. And to relieve that tension between your selves of different eras, you have a little laugh at your bygone follies. *Oh, how cute I was, how cheeky, how happy I am now, you sexy but stupid scoundrel of my youth…* And, with a wistful sigh, you measure your follies and sip your drink, somewhat comforted by how very wrong you once were.

But, what if you weren't wrong? *Archigram 9* may appear to have been a wild little booklet of *MAD Magazine* imaginings, but like all *Archigrams 1–9 1/2*, and now *10*, vital messages were dropped within the visual chaos. The vital messages in *Archigram 9*, as looney as they might've seemed then, are deadly accurate now. Read for a moment, these sentiments by Peter Cook in the introduction of 9: *Gardening and the easing of tension between the mechanical and the natural is a theme in this issue … (where) one can see the foolishness in the traditional separation of equipment, facilities … and architecture for that matter … what is needed is an all-embracing regard for* survival.

Or, this snippet that should be written immediately on every architecture text everywhere: *At this moment, effective action seems very necessary. Everywhere there is too much chat, too many people wanting to be seen to be shouting …* Better: *The old gentleman-world of the architects is crumbling.* Best: a packet of seeds to grow Night Scented Stock stapled (upper right-hand corner) to page 7.

The cover of *Archigram 9* may have seemed very hippie-ish and out-there in 1970: bright yellow with a cartoon fellow content in front of his cartoon house with his cartoon dog amid a bloom of cartoon flowers interspersed with reel-to-reel tape decks, flickering screens, and a rock voice microphone. Today, that cover, and its contents, follows every current trend in an ecological and responsible life environment: small-scale building, lots of greenery, multiple iPads, a fondness for ¼ inch analogue tape, and plenty of pet imagery.

Colin Rowe, in discussing the heroic modernist era and their dreams of reforming cities on the Hegelian terms of many Germans and one Swiss, bluntly wrote: *(Their) hoped-for condition did not ensue.* But Archigram in 1970, those crazy misfits, well, their 'hoped-for condition' was exactly what should have ensued! Perhaps, if we only listened, if we only took seriously the idea of a home filled with robots and gardening, or a room of 1,000 rooms of virtual interfaces, our humankind would be a lot less wary of the technological and environmental mandate now before us.

If only we had dropped our *Sears Catalog*, and picked up Stewart Brand's *Whole Earth Catalog*, perhaps a smaller carbon footprint, and a much fuller life, would already be mitigating climate disaster. If only we'd planted the damn seeds!

Today, an etching on a glass fishbowl, inscribed by dolphins, who have departed Earth, thanking us for all the fish, may not surprise us in the least. Our heedless inattention to our suffering planet makes any action now feel belated, and we, here, fifty-something years later, ask what can be done. Luckily, Archigram has always been about architecture (hence, the name), and architecture has a current affinity for experimentation. Listen then to Cook's 'And Then?' in *9* and hear the deep subsonic message that we still must heed.

Architecture's various technologies — the drawing, the computer rendering, the fabrication robotic interface, artificial intelligence — are the media that bring us into the *unlike and the unknown, the real and the unreal*. These media are the matter of experimentation and exploration, and the means by which we register and re-register each new reality, each new universe, each fantastic layer, as tangible, plausible, visual environments. Combine this with David Greene's, er, green programme and his interchangeable electric gardening aids (have a garden and a collection of robots), and the design of the built environment can begin to reveal a sexy and necessary future, or as Archigram stated in 1970: *We are following our dreams yet further and seeing now a gentler, softer, and more tantalising environment ... the next move is with the activist, the opportunist, and the inventor in league.*

About time we all got on with it.

'NESTY TRAVELLER'
Indonesia

Naja + deOstos

We design creatures for the future forest. We are interested in producing architecture that celebrates optimistic alternatives against stiff sustainable practices. Our project is in a threatened tropical mangrove forest in Indonesia. The design explores local narratives and contemporary technologies to create a new context for visitors to interact with and reimagine what a forest can be.

MEMORY NEST IS A CREATURE WITH A SKIN FULL OF CAVITIES that ascend upwards inviting non-human occupation. As a skin without a body, the vessel consists of patterns of rattan with pockets, tunnels, and voids to be used as non-human nests. As an installation it seeks to investigate the potential of natural rattan by increasing the biodiversity of a small mangrove island amid human visitations.

At the edge of Jakarta, Indonesia, the project is part of a long-term experiment to design a new threshold between city and forest. The design was developed utilising Indonesian master craftsmanship, digital experimentation, and biological insights into non-human habitats.

Winka

The dichotomy of nature and culture is deeply embedded in Western thought and has formed our conventional understanding of architecture as a timeless, immutable thing resisting the flux of time and matter. The Anthropocene has fundamentally altered this paradigm, and has consequently become the biggest challenge and most relevant project we will work on as architects in this century. Human activity has impacted the environment to a degree that now constitutes a distinct and observable geological change, in which human subjects have become the dominant influence on climate and the environment.

In the next wave of the Anthropocene, where climate change and environmental extremes threaten our and other species' existence, architecture must transform to remain relevant and to have positive agency over its environment. It needs to learn, adapt, and hybridise. Rather than simply applying vegetation to otherwise inert structures, buildings themselves must adopt nature's intelligence, by hybridisation and by engaging in symbiotic relationships with nature. Buildings themselves then become 'synthetic natures'. As building systems start to generate mutually beneficent, self-sustaining, and self-healing habitats and environments, they will gain agency over, and create positive feedback on the environment.

Recent research into plant intelligence has taught us how plants have an innate capability to react to environmental stresses and adapt and transform themselves to be capable of not only surviving environmental catastrophes, but also of increasing their phytoremediation capabilities, and creating another, strange new beauty. Richard Goldschmidt, a geneticist, sees this new form of evolution as radical mutants, what he terms 'hopeful monsters' in reference to a concept from evolutionary biology. Some biologists define these hopeful monsters as organisms with a profound mutant phenotype giving them the potential to establish a new evolutionary lineage more resistant to future challenges.

MONSTERS +

Such 'mutant' properties and behaviours became the inspiration for an altogether different model of buildings as hybrids, in constant exchange with their ecosystems and energy flows. This new concept of form and matter has the capacity to transform radically the very purpose and meaning of architecture. It offers the promise of a mutually beneficial coexistence of nature and architecture, environments, and bodies, defined by their symbiotic performance and behaviour rather than bio-aesthetic analogies.

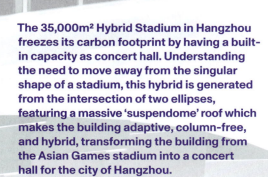

These hybrids require a new typology, or taxonomy, exhibiting a more complex set of behaviours, thus gaining a unique appearance and identity generated to be attractors and generator of future urban possibilities. Architecture as synthetic nature grows, adapts, absorbs toxins, generates energy, filters, and retains water, and promotes biodiversity. As an active generator of matter and nature, architecture thus has the capacity and responsibility to be part of the solution rather than mitigator of the problem, closer to Richard Goldschmidt's radical mutants or hopeful monsters.

The 35,000m² Hybrid Stadium in Hangzhou freezes its carbon footprint by having a built-in capacity as concert hall. Understanding the need to move away from the singular shape of a stadium, this hybrid is generated from the intersection of two ellipses, featuring a massive 'suspendome' roof which makes the building adaptive, column-free, and hybrid, transforming the building from the Asian Games stadium into a concert hall for the city of Hangzhou.

The building is not only submerged in the landscape, it also ties back into the surrounding nature; engineers designed the structure to be cooled by water extracted from newly reconstituted wetlands, and energy is preserved by only cooling the seats of the viewers while enhancing natural ventilation and lighting through upper openable vent windows and the central skylight.

MUTANTS

The building is literally INHALING and EXHALING.

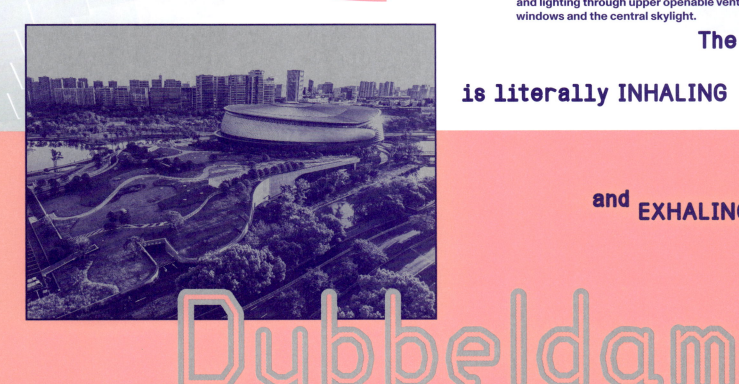

Dubbeldam

A WORLD IN TRANSITION
Odile Decq

The new technologies we already use, the algorithms that force us to move ever faster, simultaneously assist and confuse us. They have the ability to propose for us, but where is our power to imagine, create, and meet the challenges of the world in the making? What players are we and will we be tomorrow?

For many, this may be a frightening thought, but we're facing a situation reminiscent of the late 1980s, when computers first arrived on the scene. At the time, many architects rejected them, thinking that they would no longer be able to create, and yet they have all taken them in hand. So we need to tame these new ways of doing things by using AI tools. We need to keep an open mind and an open eye, so that we can harness their creative potential.

A long time ago, Archigram developed images and ideas that drew on the world in motion and the ideas in turmoil at the time, to show that it was possible to turn everything upside down, to rethink everything.

The drawing I propose is the result of an instant, a flash of imagination during a project in the making. A freeze frame and the machine made a bug. It's this bug that interests me, because it then becomes the project and shows me the future contained in the drawing we were making, which we couldn't see at the time because it was moving too quickly.

We have to watch and use what passes by fleetingly. We have to be curious and observe the world in transformation, so that we can seize it and set off on the adventure of creation with enthusiasm and without nostalgia.

But it seems to me that we might want to think about this, because in an insidious and surely unintentional way, we are witnessing the progressive erasure of the positive values of adventure in our daily lives and in our creations. Adventure is losing its appeal. We are increasingly obsessed with the idea of peril, and from the precautionary principle to excessive prudence. Fear is creeping in.

To discover is to take the risk of the unknown, the different, and sometimes the strange. Creation, like scientific research, means accepting that our certainties are called into question. To teach is to transmit, and to transmit is also to give. Schools are the last places where we give the courage to invent, where we offer the courage of imagination, and where we transmit the courage to realise.

We must go on!

People's architecture office

MEGACITY PLUGINS

Plugin Houses populate pre-existing communities built on sprawl. These prefabricated and customised interventions fill in dilapidated buildings, backyards, and rooftops. Layers of elongated platforms ascend above as a horizontal form of vertical expansion. Highways, streets, and parking lots, once storage for mostly empty private spaces, are repurposed for living. A three-dimensional network of public transport, consisting of vertical cores and suspended monorails, provides swift mobility. The thriving city is car-free, and it's okay because everything is convenient. The city is the megastructure, constantly adapting, always alive with spontaneous social activity, and continuously densifying to allow more people to live where they most want to live.

... a plugin is a ... component that adds a specific feature to an existing ... program. When a program supports plugins, it enables customization. Source: Wikipedia

ORCHID HOUSE

Featherstone Young

Orchid House is one of Lower Mill Estate's Landmark houses inspired by the rare Bee Orchid flower found at the estate.

The organic form is created from laminated veneer lumber (LVL) ribs and clad with timber shingles (tiles). The camouflage pattern is burnt into the timber. The house can be located on any lakeshore site, with the main living spaces floating over the water.

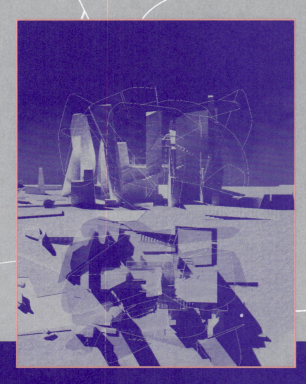

Gavin

CREPUSCULAR HOUSE

Light is easily one of modern architecture's greatest infatuations. This drive for light has created a drive for glass boxes which are entirely co-dependent on mechanical systems to maintain an environmental equilibrium. However, these lingering desires of the modern age have assumed daylight to be a universal experience, yet the modern working day means we are only in the home for two thin slivers of daylight; the crepuscular hours of dawn and dusk.

What if we created an architecture for these two moments in time? An architecture designed for this theatrical moment in the day, of elongated shards of golden light in the crepuscular hours? And what if by focusing on just these two moments of light, we could reduce the need for energy-hungry cooling systems, protecting the house from the harsh, scorching midday sun of the desert environment?

To begin, a flat site is transformed into an undulating landscape where the ground is carved out and compressed into shear walls, and baked in the scorching sun. On this landscape, towers of stone are constructed like lithic sculptures, which reveal moments of the house to come. If you look, hints of life can be spotted; a void carved out for a wardrobe, the first few steps of a staircase, and the sliced tops of the stone towers hinting at the forms that they are about to meet.

The next phase is to cover this sun-baked landscape to create a home. Overhead, unique petals come hovering in by crane, slotting precisely into their place atop and among the stone towers. These petals hold a striking form, with gentle bends, sharp folds, rounded corners, and not a right angle in sight. They jostle above the house, creating canyons and caves within. Outside, they lurch down towards the ground, covering the house to the east, west, and south. This cover is opened at just the right moments, with light piercing in through gaps and slits in and between the petals, forging brief slivers of light in the crepuscular hours.

Beyond shade, these petals complete a passive thermal system with the excavated ground below. The landscape of the ground floor is used as a thermal labyrinth that lets hot air rise and evacuate up through thermal chimneys inside the petals. The petals are adaptable to take on more active technologies such as photovoltaics for energy, or use algae-based materials to filter the air.

Crepuscular House stands as an antithesis to the universal philosophies of the modern architecture principles. It was born from CRAB Studio's methodology that blends traditional craftmanship with digital innovation. Spaces and forms initially crafted by hand are translated through scan into digital models, challenging conventional spatial paradigm. This approach creates an architecture that is uniquely intricate, beautiful, and purposeful, embracing eccentricities and disruption to redefine the potential of domestic realms.

Robotham

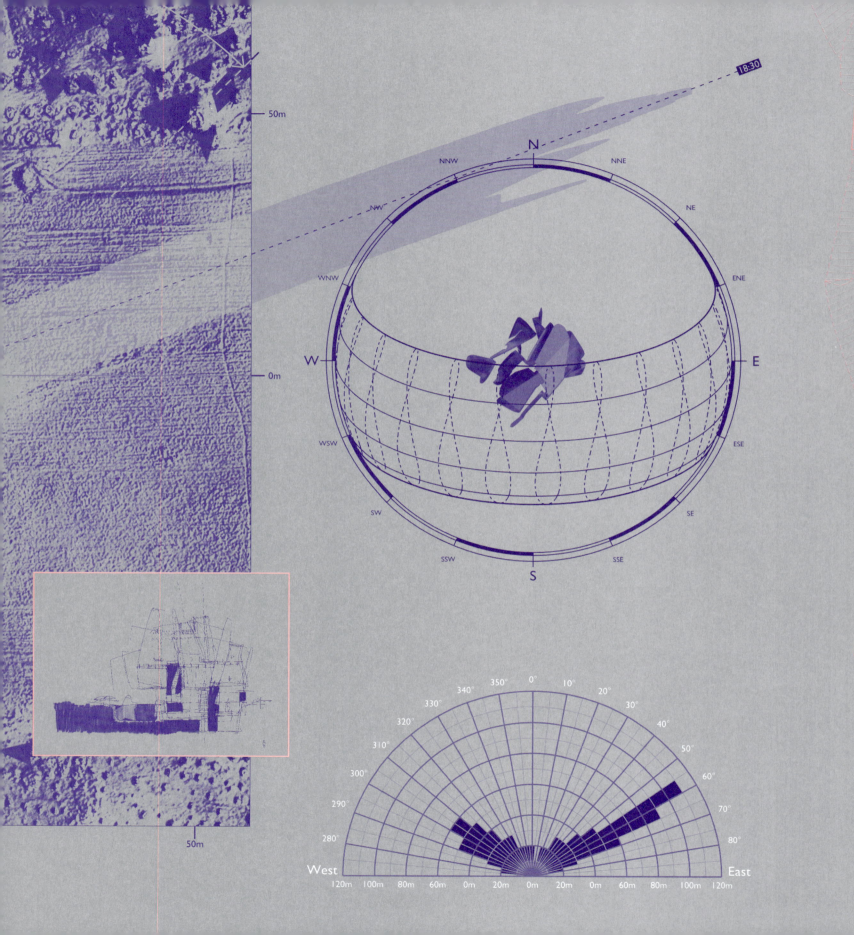

Neil Denari

SUM HOUSE 1+2

LOS ANGELES

'The sum of the parts is greater than the whole.' This inversion of a well-known aphorism is used as a guide in the development of a method for design that foregrounds discrete, highly articulated *hand-in-glove* performance criteria with respect to complex formal and spatial arrangements in architecture. Through self-similar materials, greyscale colourways, and precise alignments between diverse tectonic elements, this work speaks to *smooth differences* rather than difficult wholes. Here, nothing is artificially scaled or located arbitrarily, becoming on the one hand a what you see is what you get building and, on the other, a project that overtly obscures common architectural legibility.

Eric Owen Moss

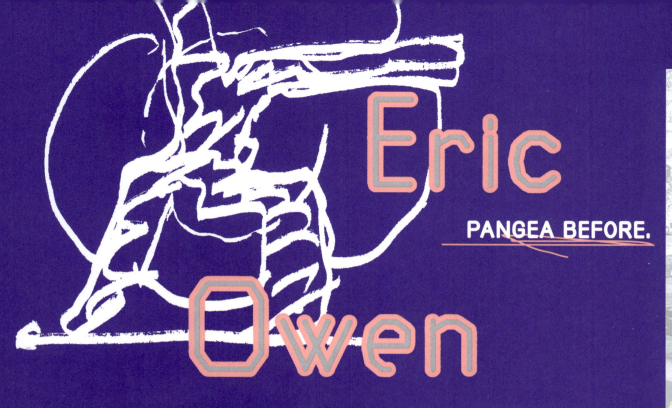

PANGEA BEFORE.

PANGEA AFTER.

BOTH.

The name Pangea represents a geological hypothesis regarding the earliest stage of the Earth's development when the land mass was a single, unified form. That single land mass subsequently divided over millennia, like a puzzle taken apart, leaving the separate continents we see today. One can observe the pieces and see how they once joined together, the edges of one reciprocating those of its opposite.

The Congress Centre concept, with reference to the Pangea analogy, originates with a cylindrical form which is then broken into parts/volumes as the programme and organisation require, leaving a clear residual form language that associates the separate parts with a conceptual whole to which, in theory, the parts could return. Likewise, the four new buildings share a subtly variable design vocabulary that suggests a consistency of form, shape, and space, notwithstanding distinctions between organisation and programme.

Design homogeneity and heterogeneity. Pangea Before. Pangea After. Both.

THE TREBINJE ARTS PARK

A 1,000-metre-long Civic, Art, and Culture Pedestrian Promenade, running east–west, conducts concertgoers, workers, residents, and visitors to five project venues — the Hotel, the Congress Centre, the Sports Complex, the Administrative Centre, and the park itself.

Each of the four buildings, roughly equidistant from one another, sits in a reflective pool. In the midst of each pool is a public plaza and building lobby, an extension of the east-west promenade. Bridging above each plaza and entry lobby, in the spirit of the three historic bridges of Trebinje, the new structures are located in the air.

Peter Cook

IN CONVERSATION WITH KATRIN FÖRSTER

KF Well, Peter, this is quite a significant moment in Archigram's history — it's fifty years since the publication of *Archigram 9 ½* and I expect most people thought that would be the last of it. Now here we are, with *Archigram 10*, which you've described as 'a poke in the eye for those people who would have us drag architecture into the boring abyss'. Maybe you could talk about some of the projects you've chosen to include, and the variety of approaches that we find in *Archigram 10*.

PC I think you're right to stress 'variety', Katrin. I tend to be attracted by two tendencies in architectural creativity: one is a project's motivation as an underlying structure — that acts as both a conceptual framework and a kind of scaffolding and is often represented as a diagram. You might say that Plug-in City and Urban Mark are the generators. The other tendency is an almost gothic manoeuvring — a weaving, with continuously developing form, likely to be a sinewy growth. Marcos Cruz, Marjan Colletti, et al., all explore biomorphic structures that evoke the gothic notion of the sublime. Yet most of the architects in *Archigram 10* don't form a particular cabal, or follow a particular mannerism. They're not from the same stable, and they are of many different ages. What they have in common is a willingness to explore. This is in contradistinction to architects who may be competent, but are habitually procedural; who don't like to explore because it 'slows things down'.

KF Exploration is a key word here. Architects and technology companies, such as ABB, know that we have to explore in order to continue to progress, and to make full use of time, energy, and resources. Not just out in the world, but also within the human body, within a person's lifetime and achievement range. You've characterised that as 'exploring the potential of the normal'.

PC The normal is what confronts us when we get up in the morning. We might ponder the weather, the efficiency of the shower, the health-giving properties of the breakfast, or the comfort of the room. Generally, these are all imperfect conditions. But most of the people included here are willing to look beyond that and ask: what is the potential of the day, of the space; what is the potential of time; what is the potential of technology?

'Architecture is in a predicament', they say. For as long as I can remember, people have been saying that architecture's finished, that it no longer has relevance. Certainly, you could argue that you no longer need an architect. Nowadays, you can simply programme an AI-assisted robot to make you a building. You just feed in lots of criteria and the result will technically be a building. It might be very good, or it might not. But like all AI things, it assumes optimal conditions, whereas the people in *Archigram* are thinking beyond the optimal. They're saying, 'Yes, we know that these optima exist but we're looking into the crevices; we're looking at the hybrid.' Not only the hybrid object, or the hybrid assembly, or the hybrid diagram, but the hybrid approach, the hybrid person. That person might be someone who trained as an engineer but is increasingly looking at paintings; or the architect who has become an engineer, or a scientist. They may even be that lost commodity — the inspired layman. All of them call upon an inner curiosity — and probably have a healthy resistance to boredom.

KF Many of the architects in *Archigram* are people who draw well, and who use drawings to develop ideas. To what extent does drawing play a role in teasing out those hybrid solutions?

PC The process of drawing can take you tangentially from an expected path. Other methodologies lack that agility, although computer drawing, harnessed to AI, can do amazing things. But computerised sequences generally follow straight paths, when what you need to do is think sideways.

Take someone like Mike Webb, on the one hand, and Mark West on the other. Much of what they do is perverse, in the sense of its unexpectedness — it is *all* sideways thinking.

Then I think it's interesting to compare Mark West with Perry Kulper. Kulper's work is peppered with a myriad of traceable references, but like a good chef he knows how to combine ingredients in new ways. West is more consistent. With him, you can trace a direct route from head to hand, even if he sometimes uses the computer. You never know what might come out of his head. It may start as something that suddenly turns into something else.

Other architects have moved slowly from the practice of constructing quite good buildings to doing absolutely extraordinary things. Take two very different people: Odile Decq and Winka Dubbeldam. They both come from fairly conventional architectural backgrounds. They both developed their practices through their own experience and intellect — *doing by doing by doing* — and now they find themselves operating as explorers.

The difference between this *Archigram* and the early ones, is that more than half the people in the publication were not born when *Archigram 9 ½* came out, in 1974. And they have grown up with a very different scenery. But they are as audacious as the earlier guys. In some ways much more audacious, because the culture surrounding them has become less and less supportive of originality. Am I deluding myself if I think people in the 1960s found originality strange but sort of *curious*? The mainstream was suspicious of it, but nonetheless allowed itself to be a little more indulgent. And then, from the 1990s onwards, the cumulative mood of moralism fed an increasingly suspicious chorus of denigration.

It has become harder to be original and perverse because the world has become mean and frightened. So if it is successful, in my terms, a lot of people will dislike this new *Archigram*. It will make them feel uncomfortable. If others just find it sort of mildly amusing, I will be disappointed but not necessarily surprised. To the optimists I am raising a banner: 'Don't be afraid!' I'm consciously targeting most of the architectural writers I know, many of the people who teach in schools, many who are in offices. Some of these pay lip service to progress, but are really reactionaries-in-hiding.

KF It's interesting to look at how much society has changed since the last *Archigram* was published, and how that transformation has affected architecture. Most of the work you've included here is by people who are or have been teachers, whereas fifty years ago I suspect it would have been by practitioners.

PC If you look very hard you might find the odd person who hasn't taught, but somehow I doubt it. One reason I invited so many people from SCI-Arc is that the school houses a disproportionate number of highly individualistic people, who are effectively in competition with each other — plus it's had a series of directors *all of whom* have been designer-architects.

The other thing that's significant about this *Archigram* (and I make no apology for the fact), is that many of the contributors are based either in London or Los Angeles. I feel the strong cultural connection between the two cities. They're both supportive of the creative individual; and they're both places in which you can 'disappear' when you want to. Unlike Paris or New York, for example, where you always have to be seen.

It's interesting to look at how the dynamics of different cities at certain points in their history affect the dynamics of practice. In Vienna, for example, in the early part of the last century, you'd have found an extraordinary mixture of guys embracing different artistic disciplines: Arnold Schoenberg making a painting, or Ludwig Wittgenstein designing a house, or architects creating furniture. Or take the syndrome in Detroit in the 1950s, when the Saarinens were at Cranbrook, and Charles Eames, Robert Venturi, Kevin Roche, Tony Lumsden, and a dozen others were popping out of the school or the Saarinen office.

Similarly, I've experienced the scene in Tokyo — my favourite *other* city — with the Metabolists and Arata Isozaki inspiring Toyo Ito and Itsuko Hasegawa, and they in turn inspiring Kazuyo Sejima and Ryue Nishizawa.

For me, the impetus comes from teaching and nurturing people and watching different talents come and go. We had a particularly creative period here in London, in the 1970s, when Zaha Hadid, Cedric Price, Archigram, Rem Koolhaas, and the high-tech guys were all buzzing around the Architectural Association. There was a tiny niche of lyricism, now almost forgotten, in which the key protagonist was Peter Wilson. Another being Christine Hawley, from whom Gavin Robotham's design mannerisms are derived. Working together with both of them, I found myself lyricising my tendency towards mechanism. Indeed, Christine and I called our stuff 'lyrical mechanism'.

I suspect that a fly on the wall could have picked up on similar niches deviating from, but being inspired by those dynamic nodes of Vienna, Detroit, or Tokyo. So the hot 'cores' and the 'niches' are more than coincidental.

Many parallels exist in key schools at special moments. A random list could include Mies van der Rohe's influence at the Illinois Institute of Technology, in the 1950s, Egon Eiermann's influence in Karlsruhe, in the 1960s, Sverre Fehn in Oslo, in the 1990s, John Hejduk at Cooper Union, in the 1980s, Kazuo Shinohara at the Tokyo Institute of Technology, in the 1980s, or Louis Kahn's legacy at the University of Pennsylvania. These inspiring individuals go far beyond pedagogy — they result in clear directions of architecture itself.

KF I like the fact that in *Archigram 10* you juxtapose work by architects who might not have been considered in that way before — such as you've done with Odile Decq and Thom Mayne.

PC I find that certain juxtapositions are suddenly very powerful. That particular combination not only looks stunning but raises many questions about architecture and its vocabulary.

You'll find some predictable relationships in these pages, and then there are others that are quite unexpected. Nat Chard and Perry Kulper have collaborated in the past and may be one of the more obvious couples. Other combinations have crept up on me. I invited Gilles Retsin and Barry Wark to take part separately, for example, but then they sent me a message saying that they wanted to work together. I would have connected Barry Wark with Marjan Colletti more instinctively, but because I don't know everybody's network, or the intricacy of those networks, I didn't make the connection. But I'm fascinated, nonetheless.

KF Another interesting juxtaposition was to group together all the people who are focused on the design of the house.

PC That group spans from those who are interested in the biomorphic, through to the geometric, or the totally conceptual. There are people who do unusual-looking houses, and weave new kinds of geometries, such as Sarah Featherstone from the English scene. I've included an experimental house that she designed ten or eleven years ago. It's the wildest thing she's done. These days she makes rather good but more circumspect cultural buildings, that have to be acceptable within the English context. She pushes it as far as she's allowed to go, but she's done nothing like this house.

So in a way I'm saying, 'Come on Sarah, remember when you did these interesting projects', whereas Gavin Robotham tends to build quite exotically relative to Sarah, so up to a point his house is an extension of *business-as-usual*. Knowing Gavin well, I know that his work is essentially sculptural — he's an extremely good form-giver.

I remember in my early experimental days, the term 'house' being a metaphor. One did a non-house, a travelling house, a plug-in house, or a capsule house, a suit-as-house. Similarly, there are many exploratory projects that attached themselves to the term 'city', though with very unusual physiognomy, so as with the house a non-city is still talking about 'city'. My more recent drawings are often called 'city', such as 'Melting City', or 'City as a Room', etc. I'm still in love with the idea of the house, or the city although not necessarily as we know them.

KF ABB has been doing interesting work in this sector at Brobyholm, in Sweden. It's a joint venture between ABB-free@home® (Building and Home Automation Solutions) and Samsung SmartThings. For the first time, all the home technologies can talk holistically to each other and work from a single app. They've created the smartest residential community in the world.

PC Very soon we'll take all these smart technologies for granted. The house will become increasingly responsive and adaptive, until it is essentially a sophisticated environment-creation system. We'll all look out through windows that can simulate sunlight, or transform into television screens, or simply change the scenery if asked to. The electronic house may take many different forms. You might specify one that allows you to indulge a passion for opera, and can simulate a chorus behind you so that you can pretend you're a diva. Another might be configured to reveal a fully equipped gymnasium. Another might be geared up so that you can breed chickens and live in it as well. Anything is possible.

I would love to design such a thing. And that's where companies like ABB need to engage with designers who are capable of original thinking, and vice versa. Otherwise they're just providing tech-support for yet more bourgeois suburban houses. But once designers know what's being developed, and what's possible, to reciprocate we have to say: 'Okay, you've invented a thing that makes a roof into a floor whereby we get radiant heat; we don't have a heater, we don't even have a switch. *Okay*, you can do that, but can you do it bigger? Can you do it out in the garden?' That kind of dialogue gives you a marvellous canvas for operations. One dilemma, however, is that the technological triggers of these things *don't look like anything* — whereas the 'chamber' or 'enclosure' obviously does.

Moving further forward, we're talking not just about how smart technologies impact the design of the house and the concept of shelter, but also how they might change the ways in which communities sustain themselves. I don't mean the current concept of 'sustainability', but actual systems — infrastructure. I think what will happen to urbanism is very significant, since most people now live in large urban conglomerates. We will move from the scale of the autonomous house to the scale of the autonomous town, or city.

KF So, Peter, we've talked about *Archigram 10*, but where do we go from here: if you were to do *Archigram 11*, how would it be different?

PC If there is a future *Archigram* after number 10, I will be very interested in it taking another new direction, as I did with *Archigram 5*. After the first four publications, which were essentially free-form, we took one big idea and addressed urbanism and the metropolis. Then in subsequent issues we went back to free-form and in *Archigram 9* even homed-in on gardening.

Were I to do another *Archigram*, I might not include anyone who's appeared in this one. Possibly, I might ask each person to nominate somebody younger than themselves, who might not be doing what they do. Or in some other way trawl people from a different context.

Some of the more experienced contributors (and by 'experience' I mean being not necessarily older, but those who've done more than one thing), interest me because they've worked in real practice also, have been involved in building a new town, or an urban project of some sort. I'm also interested in a wider context, with people whose investigations are related to industry — people who've invented things, or developed a production technique. I'm interested in how processes inform other processes, and how one can make tangential leaps from one discipline to another. Whatever *Archigram* is, or means, it has to be a *provocation*.

KF Thank you, Peter, for such a fascinating conversation, and for pointing us to the future.

PC Thank you Katrin! And huge thanks also to ABB for making *Archigram 10* possible.

The Biocene House is a prototype of our future human habitat. Through a novel typology, the home will become a fluid space that supports care. For example: the dynamics of adult relationships, raising children, incorporating multiple generations, as well as the locus where we begin caring for our environment.

The facade is composed of 'villi' creating folds that maximise surface area for exchange with biodiversity in the house's immediate surroundings. Bio-integrated design enables the building to be sensitive to its ecology and inhabitants. Performative qualities such as bioremediation of greywater are embedded in the building fabric.

Healthy microbiomes are supported through bioreceptive materials and food cultivation, enhancing wellbeing. New methods of low-carbon construction are examined through bio-based composites created from photosynthetic processes. The Biocene House enables us to imagine our lives as part of fundamentally connected ecosystems, shaping how we share resources in future.

The **BIOCENE HOUSE** is a prototype of our future human habitat

Marcos Cruz

Marjan Colletti's Postdigital Practices aim to transcend the limitations of an outdated digital paradigm, upgrading and embedding it within a twenty-first-century context. These practices explore the integration of digital technologies with biological, ecological, and material sciences, as well as traditional craftsmanship, to create innovative and adaptive architectural solutions. This transdisciplinary approach enables the creation of works that are both conceptually rich and materially sophisticated; it thus challenges the binary distinction between the digital and the analogue, instead embracing a continuum where digital processes and material outcomes inform and enhance each other. By integrating diverse disciplinary fields, from art and agriculture to fashion and science, postdigital practices strive to create a new architectural ethos that is creative and proactive, environmentally conscious, and technologically advanced.

Leveraging 2D drawing techniques, 3D modelling and additive manufacturing printing technologies, 4D advanced simulation/animation tools, AI and robotic fabrication, postdigital architectural practices seek to foster a more intricate, responsible, and symbiotic relationship between the built environment and the natural environment, promoting unexpected hybrid techno-environmental architectural prototypes. This vision fosters a harmonious coexistence between human-made structures and natural processes, redefining conventional roles and responsibilities within all creative practices.

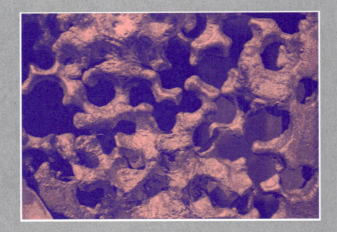

POSTDIGITAL PRACTICES

Marjan Colletti

EcoLogic Studio

TALLINN

WET CITY

is a symbiotic anti-city.

It co-evolves present-day Tallinn

to redefine its entire urban metabolism.

The Paljassaare Peninsula, at the outskirts of Tallinn, is shaped by two forms of conflicting ideology: environmentalism that strives to maintain the site in a state of wilderness (the peninsula is included in the Natura 2000 network of protected areas), and commercial development that envisions its urbanisation into a green city. Both narratives are ideologically conservative in their reading and understanding of the true nature of the site. ecoLogicStudio's proposal challenges such conservative sentiments with a masterplan intended to promote a new urban morphogenesis, whereby Tallinn's actual urban wastewater infrastructure affects the biotic substratum of the peninsula.

The resulting 'contamination' becomes a morphogenetic force, inducing an artificial hyper-articulation of the landscape and its living systems which evolve into an urban digestive apparatus. Pathogens are re-metabolised, diluted, or captured by augmented ecosystems; infrastructural networks thicken into filtering surfaces, which in turn fold into an epidermis populated by a large amount of inhabitable bioreactor cells, the Anthropocene Islands of Paljassaare.

The ground protocol proposes the morphological hyper-articulation of the existing landscape and its living systems. Constantly monitored via satellite, this synthetic urban landscape feeds back to Tallinn's wastewater network in real-time. Each molecular transaction has its spatial location, morphological effect, informational address, and eco-systemic value. Satellite data is provided at a resolution of 10 × 10 metres for an area of 3 × 3 km framing the peninsula. Each pixel represents a degree of biochemical activity, defined as 'wetness', and computed with the Normalized Difference Water Index algorithm. The resulting gradient is indexed at specific locations along its ISO lines at a resolution of 2 metres. In each location, tendency lines are computed; longest lines appear in areas of highest difference in wetness or biological activity. Such locations possess maximum potential for thickening and articulating into biochemical reactors.

These prototypical bundles for wastewater purification and sludge bio-digestion are equipped with active biotechnological units; the system is monitored in real-time, sending information about the status of its internal metabolism and receiving updates from the wastewater treatment network. Its operations are constantly altered and adjusted by distributed sensing/digging robots, the cyber worms. The articulation of the existing landscape determines directions of flow and purification; in areas where the concentration of active bio-digesters is high and their emissions of heat and nutritious soil reach a critical mass, new microclimates and related habitats are formed. Growing plants, insects, and birds are attracted and become active agents of urban transformation.

Michael Webb

WHILE UNDER CONSTRUCTION

An article of faith among the six of us in Archigram was the conviction that most buildings were interesting-looking while under construction, and equally so while being demolished. It was the time in between the two events that was problematic. Buildings that just sat around doing nothing …

Hence this image of a building being constructed. Or maybe it's a scene from quotidian life, the couple living here having ordered extra living space for a weekend guest shortly to arrive. Off the edge of the picture is an on-site manufacturing machine producing floor units. A stack of four of the units, hinged so as to unfold, is shown rolling along a horizontal structural member, opening out like metal petals as it moves.

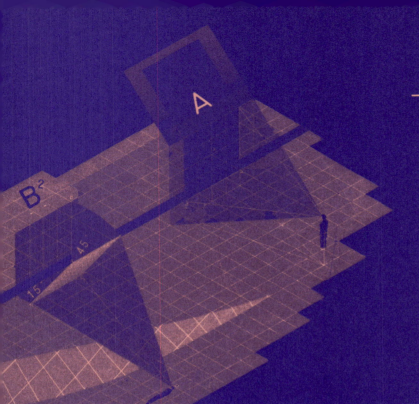

Cyclopean observer

(the single eye of conventional perspective drawing), his or her centre of vision collinear with a perpendicular emanating from the centre point of one of the unfolding panels, maintains that spatial relationship for the duration of the unfolding sequence, resulting in wild gyrations for the hapless observer.

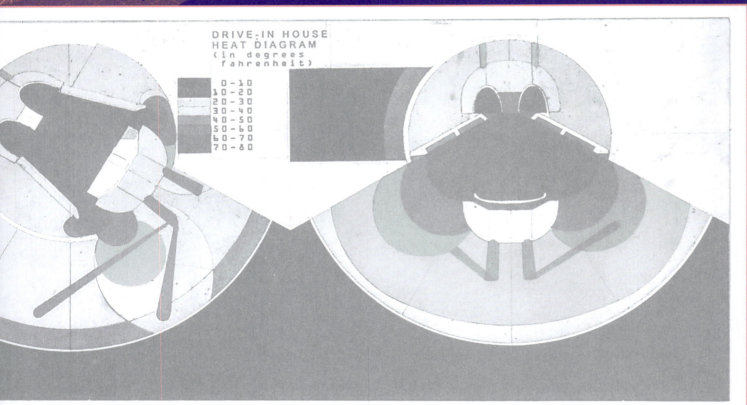

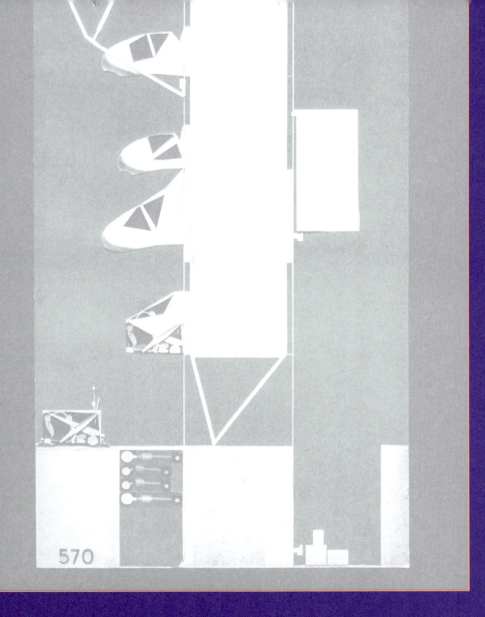

570

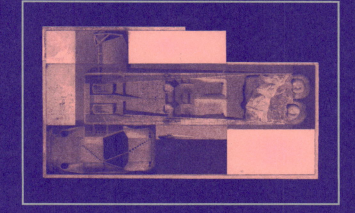

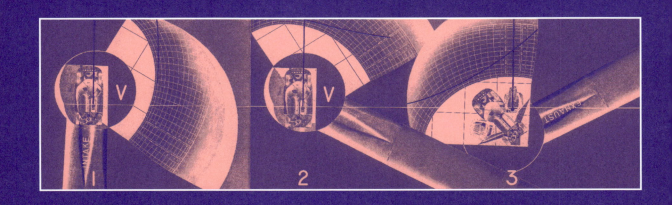

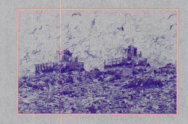

RETHINKING

David Greene

FUTURE

Beetle-mounted camera streams insect adventures

Researchers have developed a tiny wireless camera that is light enough to be carried by live beetles.

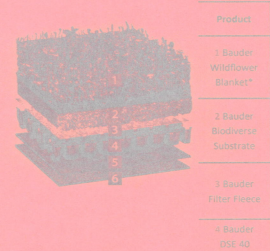

BAUDER
SYSTEM SUMMARY
Bauder WB Wildflower Bla...

Biodiverse wildflower green roof system

The pre-grown native wildflower blanket, allows the quick establishment of a green ro... British native wildflowers with less than 10% grass species, designed... long flo... compliant. This system is suitable for both new build construction... or refurbi... Roof Promise" is available for this system.

Product	Description
1 Bauder Wildflower Blanket*	Inclu... ative wil... herb... with less than 10% RHS... erfect for...
2 Bauder Biodiverse Substrate	Lightw... owing bioddi... roof pl mar... to GRO line... to BS86...
3 Bauder Filter Fleece	Filtr... hat prev fine... ing into and... e layer.
4 Bauder DSE 40 Drainage Layer	DSE 40... weight and d... layer n recycle...
5 Bauder	is 100%... Polyes...

Wheel.me robot wheels move furniture via voice commands

A Norwegian start-up wants to make it possible to rearrange a home's furniture solely via a voice command or the touch of an app's button.

To achieve this, Wheel.me has developed the Genius robotic wheels, which attach to the base of tables, chairs and other furnishings.

It is showing off a prototype at the CES tech expo in Las Vegas, where founder Atle Timenes arranged a demo for BBC Click's Lara Lewington.

Find out what else will be on show at CES 2020

See more at **Click's website** and **@BBCClick**

🕐 06 Jan 2020

f M 🐦 ✉ < Share

ARCHITECTURES

Elin... well who are the team?... I don't think we have met, perhaps we might one day?... in the past Peter was the creative impetus behind the very varied issue which often had a theme... is it weird shit still...?... What is the format? How many will be printed... if indeed it is on paper, is it? or like Abba's greatest hits presented in new media? (...) As you know Elin, Archigram originally was a pamphlet with a very small audience and the first one reviewed in the AJ as lacking any rational thought... as I guess so is this email. (...)

VOTE NOW IN OU...

ICON... SEAS

Pedro Pitarch

THE CITY OF THE CAPTIVE EVENT

is devoted to the constant construction of enclosed contexts.

It materialises the contemporary interchangeability between the artificial and the natural, as both are understood here as cultural constructions.

The long tradition of music festivals enabled the definition of an urban type that can now be inhabited by other metropolitan programmes. A city in which festivals and events of the most diverse natures are produced simultaneously next to each other. A work festival. A myth festival. An affection festival. A political festival. An infrastructural festival. A health festival …

The necessity for detachment from any existing reality led the architects of the city to a location that is the ultimate medium for abstraction: the water. Floating on pontoon-like structural systems, the city would have no context but itself. It would enable the future events to develop freely with no restrictions from a pre-existing context, territory, or society.

Located in the most artificial region of the world, the Netherlands, the city represents the Dutch obsession for the control of the environment. It floats on the main lake of Beulakker Wijde inside the domains of the Weerribben-Wieden National Park in Steenwijkerland, Overijssel.

Within the City, each event restructures the entire reality where it is performed. Everything is somehow thoroughly different. The radical social relevance of the event relies on its momentary transcendental ethos.

The frame
As buoyant platoons, the frames can be relocated when required. Each one is interchangeable and mobile, and equipped with landing piers, vertical communication cores, and general facilities.

(BB2070)
AN ATLAS
OF METROPOLITAN
ISLANDS
FOR BERLIN

New-Südkreuz

In cities like Berlin, the strong sense of community among citizens crosses the boundaries between the micro and the macro, between the global and the local. Faced with many European cities where urban developments around infrastructural nuclei are based on what is known as Transit Oriented Developments (TOD), Gross Berlin expands this concept by superimposing it with its marked social heterogeneity to generate Transit Oriented Communities. New-Südkreuz is one such example.

As a consequence, a series of Urban Domesticities unfold. A diversity of programmes and domestic uses that, freed from the traditional restrictions of the home environment, populate urban spaces.

The masterplan is completed with a catalogue of action protocols on the Urban Voids so characteristic of Berlin. We have a series of strategies for the community use of four categories of voids: abandoned lots, courtyards, residual spaces, and disused infrastructure.

Thom Mayne

Gardening Between the Mechanical and the Natural

Archigram 9 dreamt of a future 'where machines and natural forms live together, independently responding to people', an indication of the future importance of the garden. 'Gardening and the easing of tension between the mechanical and the natural' was the theme of that issue … 'what we need is an all-embracing attitude regarding survival and sustenance'.

The issue included a packet of seeds, Night-Scented Stock, *Matthiola longipetala*, having very fragrant lilac or purplish flowers followed by forked, elongated seed pods. Mattioli, an Italian botanist, cultivated these flowers thinking they promoted love and lust due to their strong scent, a spicy vanilla with an undertone of rose. The seed, being the fertilised matured ovule that contains an embryonic plant, stores material and has a protective coat.

A half century later, the garden can be seen as a generative, sometimes dominant force as a departure point for our work, allowing us to rethink the conventional model of architecture in favour of an architecture conceived to co-exist with landscape. The manipulation and understanding of biological systems and the underlying principles of behaviour and evolution play a significant role in design-thinking, leading to organisational systems that exhibit the specific traits, functions, and behaviours guided by predictable patterns of behaviour that emerge from simple rules and interactions mimicking or enhancing natural processes. Recognising that nature is constructed, we reconceive the ways that ground's morphology provokes the convention of an autonomous architecture.

As we locate multiple grounds and blur the boundaries between where one begins and the other ends, architecture approaches a mixture of the natural and the constructed. Everything is to some extent synthetic, blurring the line between building and site, urban and rural, internal and external.

BEAUTY IS DEAD

LONG LIVE BEAUTY

Craig Hodgetts

Thoughts on

Eric Owen Moss's (W)rapper

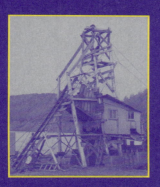

Okay, I get it. It's in the eye of the beholder. But who is that, anyway? There's been quite a churn recently, maybe not so much as the imbroglio over the stage-right entry of post-postmodern ideas, but unsettling at least. The rumbles began at the schools, well before various big guns were speaking up. But what began as a big question has now got the attention of institutions and even governments, with multiple attempts to legislate some sort of oversight to rein in architectural imagery both here in the US and jolly Anglo-Terra.

Has no one anything better to do?

Time was architects and clients alike toed the line. What was good for the goose was good for the gander. But now it seems that the guardians have fallen asleep at their posts and we (that is those who care at all about the state of affairs in architectural la-la land) have lost our resolve. I've got to wonder, actually, if it's anyone's business. To be sure, we'd all prefer to swan about in an environment that offers visual pleasures as well as a confirmation of our personal value system, but it's a fact that aside from a few neighbourhood cranks, and holiday-makers, no one pays much attention to anything higher than a lamp post, and there is no dearth of visual stimulation in the fashionistas who populate the pavements.

So what is it that has created such a logjam of opinion?

It's the lack of 'standards', which one must admit, have fallen pretty low across the board, whether it's in official debate, entertainment, or personal conduct. 'But ... but ... but' we stammer, we architects are above all that.

The very conceit of beauty, of course, lives in a fog of ego and narcissism, often used as a weapon, or term of derision for vapid, thinly disguised, hollow performers, or hurled in irony, but rarely used in art criticism, while its antonym has rarely if ever appeared in print.

What we do know is that beauty and its antonym have duelled throughout history, depending on the fickle standards of the day. Today, as the fashionistas' fascination with torn jeans, dystopian raiments, and Mad Max paraphernalia competes with gender stereo-types, bling and ultra-flash, the question has to be: whose beauty? Certainly, in a spec-trum stretching from wabi-sabi to totalitar-ian order, there is room for a bit of wear and tear. Displaced cladding, errant fastenings, and worn coatings have an often celebrated, legitimate beauty. Character, rather than nubile skin, often endures while glamour fades. Just think of the coal bunkers celebrated by Bernd and Hilla Becher that used to dot the landscape, or for that matter the graceful blades of contemporary windmills. Are they not the essence of streamlined beauty? NIMBY! And of course there's the very English James Stirling's work that Nik Pevsner called 'rude'. Very, very NIMBY! And now it's 'The (W)rapper' — Not! In! My! Back! Yard! — Ever.

I must admit that I'm a bit worn out and confused.

The glistening skins that have come to define the contemporary urbanscape are in large part a passive response to the coincidence of materials marketing, thermal and engineering necessity, and corporate identity, rather than the result of a vibrant architectural culture. If we were talking about music, our cities would be made up of what's heard in the confines of lifts, not the rowdy sounds of the arena.

One bit of rowdy design that I have personally championed, but the dogs have set upon, is known as 'The (W)rapper'. Its design seems to revel in exercising what can be done with simple stuff like steel and glass to knock a hole in the curse of beauty. Pretty, even, it ain't. Although a virtuoso exercise in structural expression, with column-free floors supported by curving members, 'logic and proportion' according to the Airplane song, 'have fallen sloppy dead!' Sometimes awkwardly fused to a vertiginous cliff of escape stairs, and wrapped in heavy straps, with a nearly prehistoric visage, it is the Godzilla of buildings, something to be reckoned with, lest it trample the nearby Metro line.

It used to be that experimentation was a given among those in our stable ... accolades went to those who pushed the envelope, whose radical aesthetic sensibility quickened our pulse and opened our eyes to unrecognised beauty; who had the guts to push concrete, steel, and glass to the limits, to run at the front of the pack; but in today's woke climate it seems that obeisance, humility, and a servile persona are prerequisites for acceptance as an architect. It's a given that a 'make no waves' posture is good business. Disruption forces realignment of more than supply chains — it jostles journeymen and thinkers alike. There is no antidote for an infection which can jam synapses, rattle juries, even, who knows, threaten the Academy and its critical journals, forcing them to be on their guard.

Now, aesthetic complaints aside, a block-by-block shootout would upend capital 'A' architectural culture at the least, with territorial skirmishes routing last century's genteel spat over post-postmodernism's step into the limelight. The larger point here is that our architectural culture needs a stick up it. Far from reflecting the values of the mainstream, in the larger cultural / aesthetic context it's an outlier, made most evident by the huge following generated by rap, goth, and cyber heroes, that the conformity demanded by the mainstream has become too stifling. The flagrant displays of rebellious fashion, personal traits, and status indicate cracks in the dominant culture's high regard for polish over substance. Architecture's day job, after all, is simply to keep the rain and vermin out, anything else of artistic or aesthetic note is quite simply superfluous, so please spare me the moans and groans about The (W)rapper.

I'm personally offended that our hatcheries have become targets for ultra conservatives to batten down the hatches and declare a moratorium on aesthetic challenges. Instead, lets commend Moss on his staying power, his willingness to put himself and his imagination on the line, his willingness to inject thoughtful, hard-won innovation rather than abject conformity into the landscape. After all, it's only design. Isn't it?

After all,

it's only design.

Isn't it?

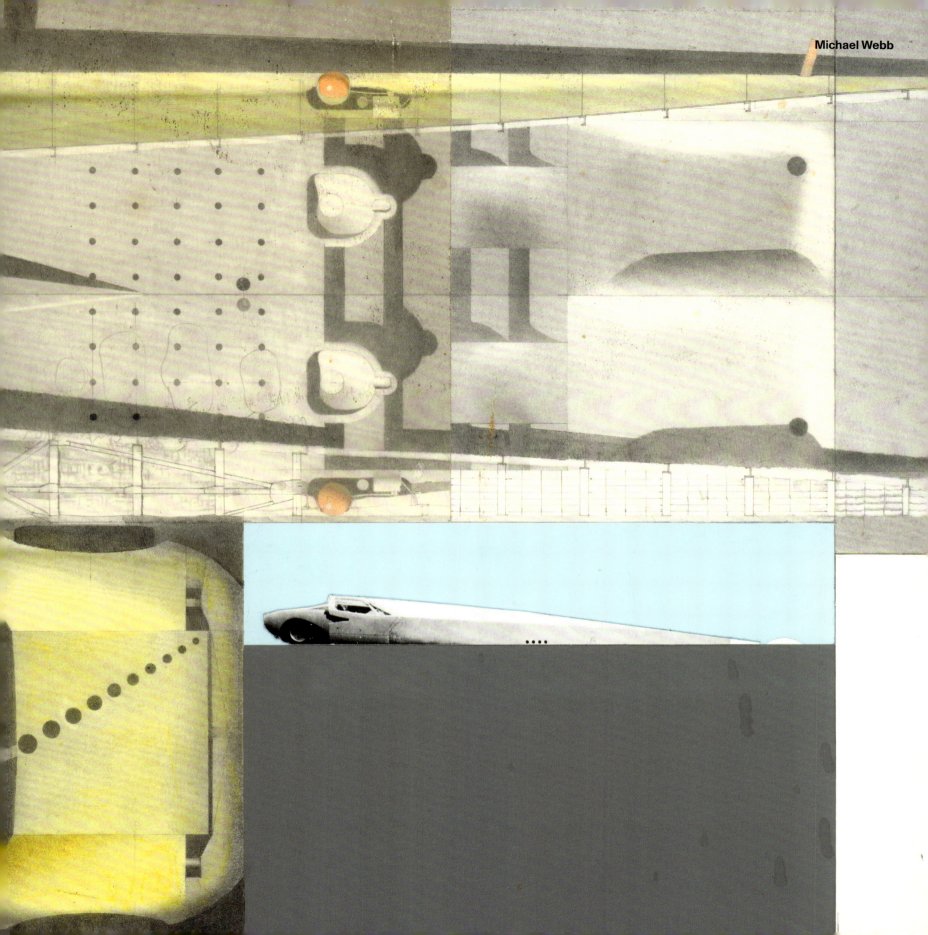

Thom Mayne

Trevor Boddy

One of the great secrets of recent visual culture is that the global social media phenomenon of Instagram could never have occurred without the pioneering of Archigram, begun half a century earlier. Not only did Archigram trigger the orgy of imagery that fills our phones, but its rules of visuality have rolled out to shape the very feeds that greet us every morning. In essence, Instagram is Archigram, transposed to new, even quicker, and more pervasive formats.

Consider the linguistic similarities between the two, their GRAMmars, so to speak. Both of these communication formats (and yes, Archigram is more about communication than conventional building) are dedicated to the primacy of the visual. Both are drained of narrative — the powerful image, pulsing with colour and mashups of the natural with the mechanical, is all that matters. Advancing the parade of images with every stroke on the little handheld screen, one comes quickly to expect the unexpected — just like Archigram.

The discontinuity of each marcher in this parade of pictures is the very point, the narrow narrative of the thing. Here a holiday spot, there an atrocity, again a pet, often a presser, even more often an unfunny joke, here comes nostalgia in faces, then futurism in devices, finish with a sunset whenever and wherever you want. Both Instagram and Archigram are relentless, relentlessness being their very point. For each, titles are but cue cards, not explanations, being merely triggers within each of their realms. Walking Cities is all you need to know from the world of words, everything else is explained by the drawings, and the drawings alone. How many Instagram captions can you remember a week later, five minutes later?

Think of the emphatic placelessness of both Instagram and Archigram. For example, a stunning shot of a voluptuous new interior comes up on the screen, but no other information is offered by the person posting it — not site, not designer, not client, not even motivation for posting it. Thus begins the erotic seduction of Instagram's comment streams, which are not unlike exploring the complex details of an Archigram montage: always 'Where?', then a meek 'Designer?', an engaging 'You there?', and often a desperate dive for personal connection: 'This reminds me of …'

Interrogations like these are the source of both pleasure and frustration in dealing with a feed of postings or a well-fed architectural drawing. Much foolishness is written about the supposed surreality, even surrealism of Archigram proposals. This is because Archigram then, like Instagram now, is a complete world unto itself — checking the bolts of linkage into reality is pointless, as the doors have slipped off this Boeing long ago. The emotion that fuels the flights of both Instagram and Archigram is a curiosity about 'The Next'. Endorphins will be triggered by the right combination of forms; it is just a matter of teasing them out of the infinite feed.

Keep going, something prompting a smile or a frown will surely come up.

The other foolishness written about Archigram is their supposed futurism. Real futures are invisible, unexpected, arriving in surprising crates with no evident bill of lading from a shipper. Produced when Britain was among the first of nations to deindustrialise, there is a heavy dose of nostalgia for the mechanical in Archigram. The buildings proposed by Archigram are at essence a kind of steam punk nouveau, wrapped in spaceship imagery triggered by Jack Kirby Marvel drawings and endless machine catalogues. Machines, please note, not the invisible sources of software. Computer code is notoriously difficult to represent in imagery, so this scenography of the recent past replaces them. And of course, this timelessness and placelessness is the reason why we love Archigram and Instagram so much. Our affection is secure and ultimately monogamous, because they are the very **same thing**.

Izaskun Chinchilla

HOW MUCH LIFE CAN YOU FIT IN A BLACK LINE?

There is a way of making architecture that consists of subdividing the available space into enclosures by means of black lines. Its followers argue that what is important is the transcendent and heroic space that remains inside the dark striations. For them, it doesn't matter if a couple of forests in Latin America are deforested to get a vault in the right proportion. The users, affected, inhabitants, passers-by, or citizens do not count until the end and if they receive buildings they dislike it is because they '*must be re-educated*'.

This is the architecture still practised by a certain number of professionals, although it has been mortally wounded since at least the 1960s. The '60s made us see that under every apparently innocent decision of theestablished powers there was an imposed political, social, and intellectual model, to which we were forced to adapt. We realised that those who had been powerless until then could build their voice and raise alternative structures. The world ceased to belong to architects, doctors, or heads of state and began to be disputed by diverse collectives.

Archigram played a leading role in this liberation. The black line lost its abstraction and its technocratic philosophy. Enclosures were now generated by components at the disposal of the user, which could be personalised and changed over time. Widows, teenagers with dependent children, single women, and the elderly, among many others, could choose how to sleep, listen to music, have fun, work, or get to know each other better. They could change their ideas and needs over time, and the cities and their architecture belonged to them for the first time, even if only partially.

Since then, an important part of architecture has broken away from a profoundly univocal and conservative way of thinking that has fewer and fewer followers. We find the single path, the dogma intolerant, because many of us know that within the black lines there is not only geometric composition and lowly cultural elitism, there can also be life — life led by the diverse inhabitants who express themselves with joy, anxiety, and drive. As revolutionaries do.

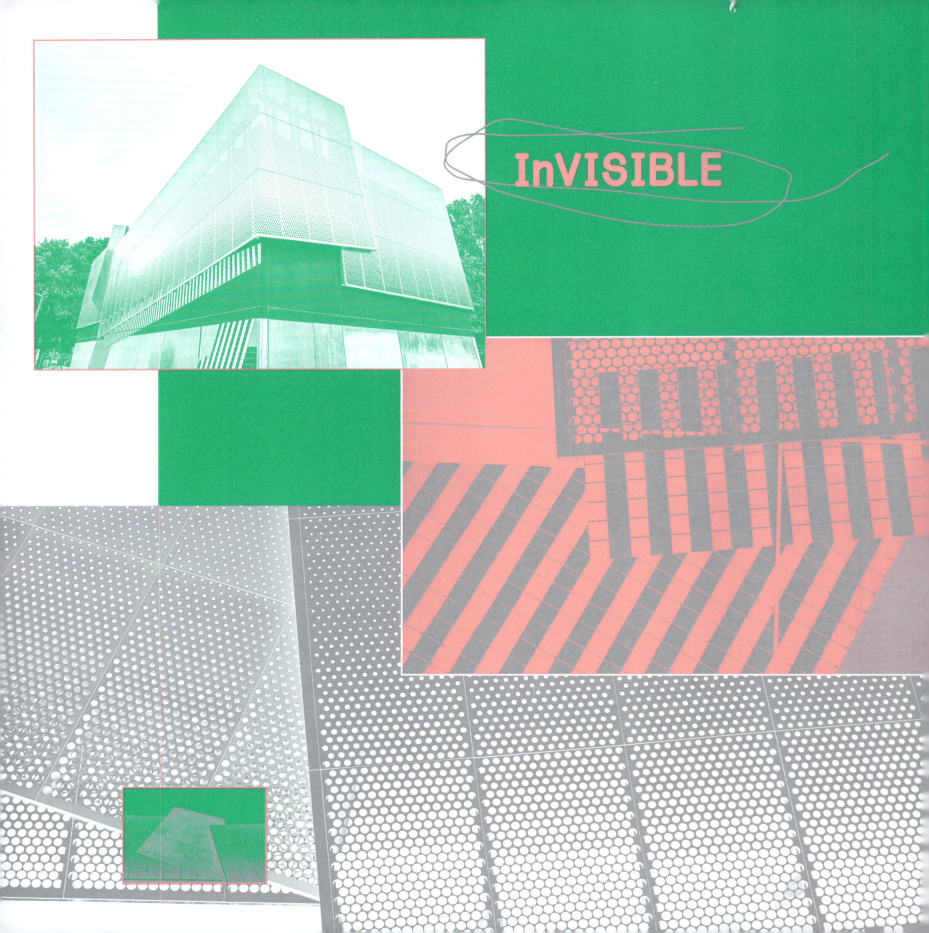

The *inVISIBLE* Dominion Energy Crystal Substation is a project that began in 2021 and was completed in 2024. Located in Crystal City, the substation was commissioned by Dominion Energy and designed by Atelier Manferdini, Los Angeles, CA. The project was led by Elena Manferdini, who brought a unique artistic and architectural perspective to the substation design.

inVISIBLE visualises the creation and distribution of electric power — an unseen, yet essential, aspect of our lives. The design draws inspiration from Manferdini's fascination with the immersive effects of vast fields of colour. The colourful facade engages viewers and prompts them to reflect on their relationship with electricity and its fundamental role in daily life.

The facade of the substation is divided into two distinct, expansive fields stacked horizontally, creating a dynamic visual narrative. On the lower half of the facade, three different sizes of colourful ceramic tiles represent a buzzing electric field. The relationships between the 2, 4, and 6-inch tiles reference the substation's main function of converting voltage from high to low or vice versa. This transformation is crucial for the efficient and safe distribution of electricity, making the varying tile sizes a fitting metaphor for the substation's operational processes.

The upper half of the facade is an immense monochrome field of metal panels that represents a folded sky. The folded design of the metal panels adds a sense of depth and dimensions, creating an interplay of light and shadow that changes throughout the day. In creating *inVISIBLE*, Manferdini, an Italian-born artist, designer, architect, and engineer, invites viewers to consider their relationship to the unseen and fundamental force of electricity. The colourful ceramic tiles and the monochrome metal panels create a dialogue between seen and unseen. Manferdini encourages viewers to contemplate the processes and tools involved in generating and distributing electricity.

inVISIBLE is a unique project that merges art, architecture, and technology. Through this project, Manferdini emphasises the importance of electricity in our lives while celebrating the aesthetic and symbolic potential of architectural design. By blending functionality with artistic expression, the project exemplifies how industrial utilitarian facilities can be reimagined to an urban environment. Therefore, it not only serves its primary function of managing electrical voltage, but also acts as a visual and conceptual exploration of the unseen forces that shape our world.

Atelier Manferdini

David Garcia

The number of tours to the exclusion zone in Chernobyl and the surrounding area has grown exponentially since the fall of the USSR. From locals to the faraway curious, newly emerging interest groups have pushed the definitions of tourism, turning this landscape into something between an archaeological site and a theme park of catastrophe.

During our visits, the severity and impact of events following the disaster became more than just a phenomenological experience. Fear of the invisible radiation shifts, of dust, of what one might inhale or accidentally touch, conditioned our every movement. Our encounters with some of the survivors and evacuees, as well as the scientists and experts still active at the site (3,000 still work in the vicinity of the reactor to this day), underlined the continuing danger to the region and beyond. Some of the buildings in Pripyat (the workers' town erected near Chernobyl in 1970) are now collapsing, placing tourists at even greater risk, and the sarcophagus enclosing the unstable Reactor 4 is itself in a fragile state.

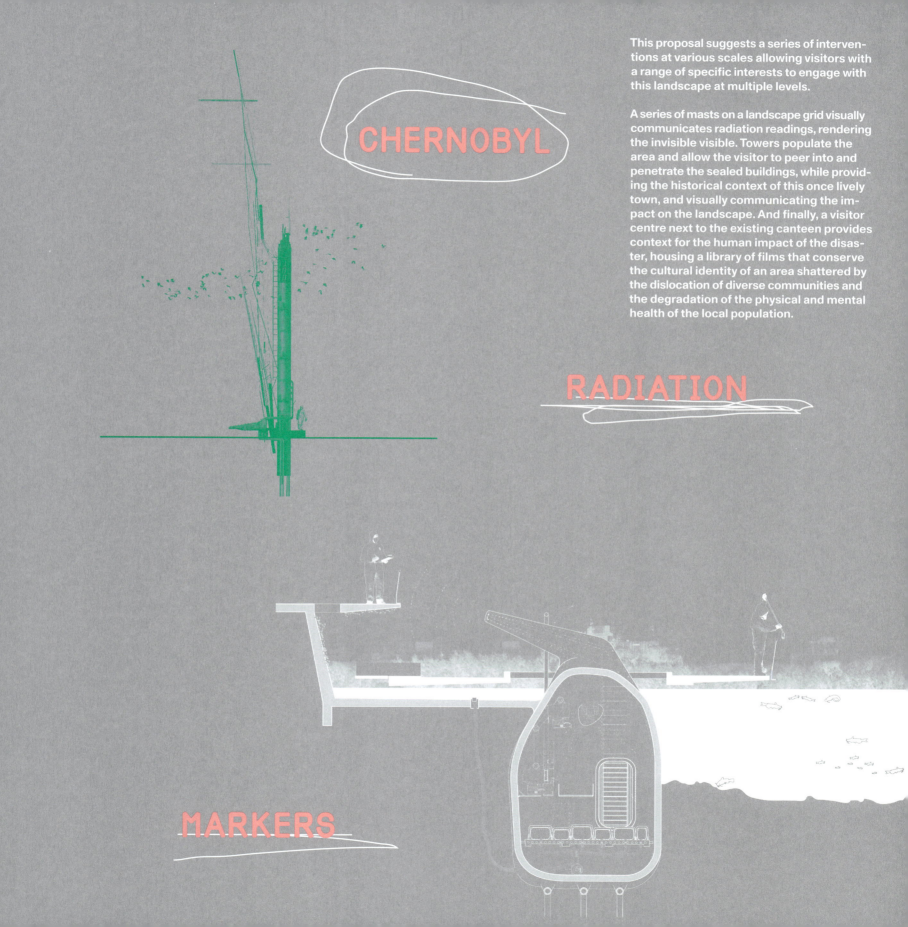

CHERNOBYL

RADIATION

MARKERS

This proposal suggests a series of interventions at various scales allowing visitors with a range of specific interests to engage with this landscape at multiple levels.

A series of masts on a landscape grid visually communicates radiation readings, rendering the invisible visible. Towers populate the area and allow the visitor to peer into and penetrate the sealed buildings, while providing the historical context of this once lively town, and visually communicating the impact on the landscape. And finally, a visitor centre next to the existing canteen provides context for the human impact of the disaster, housing a library of films that conserve the cultural identity of an area shattered by the dislocation of diverse communities and the degradation of the physical and mental health of the local population.

The contemporary architect needs to be many architects;

SURFACE ALGORITHMS

Augmenting the 600-year-old dominance of linear perspective, the picture plane, and the 'subject' position, or station point — and their historical, disciplinary, ethical, and operational consequences — is productive. Three characteristics establish this project: producing innovative visualisations while discovering and harvesting their generative potential; implementing diverse design methods to increase one's design versatility; and enlarging the conceptual frameworks through which we might imagine spatial realms. Advocating spatial visualisations, digital, manual, or combinatory, as operational compasses helps to work at these edges, all the while expanding disciplinary boundaries. This approach reinforces a belief that the architect must be many architects, a kind of metaphorical Swiss-Army knife.

Many influences have productively effected these ambitions, including: curiosity cabinets that gather things that don't naturally belong together; baroque developments in theatre, painting, and architecture; Dutch Golden Age paintings and their relational entanglements; surrealism and dadaism for their varied operational tactics that challenge default assumptions; Robert Venturi's *Complexity and Contradiction in Architecture* and relations of architecture to history, to the capacities of ambiguity, and to his 'both/and' provocation; analogical relations to Matthew Barney's *Drawing Restraint* series, where the production of obstacles makes it difficult to maintain familiar creative habits; visionary, or speculative architecture for visualising what might be possible; and Wallace Stevens' seminal poem, *13 Ways of Looking at a Blackbird*, that acts as a metaphorical cartography for conceptual and operational navigation.

an agile cultural agent

prepared to act differently

in various situations.

Creative practice must be an active construction, while undergoing constant transformation. Here, objectives might parallel those of design thinking — developing innovative working techniques to engage loosely defined and diverse ideas, through motivating the architectural drawing as materialised research. Historically, the agency and instrumentality of conventional architectural drawing types is profound. But they may not always be appropriate for certain ideas, approaches, and kinds of work. Adjusting working tactics and strategies to design more effectively may require invented representation techniques and even design methods.

To engage a wide range of subjects, my production includes fast, slow, and in-between drawings. The fast drawings are *Landscapes*, some of which are included here. I've made 750 of them. Digitally produced counterparts, the *Speculative House, Garden + Landscape* series, was produced in Photoshop, number 155. The slow drawings are more comprehensive, more deliberate. They are mini cosmologies, a world of ideas and spatial speculations, openly wondering about a project's potential.

Tailoring techniques and methods to pursue an appropriate fit between what's being worked on and how it's being worked on remains critical. In addition to using conventional drawings, one can use other kinds of drawings that are phase, or task specific. Some can be more abstract, some more figurative, and others might use multiple languages of representation, simultaneously. Some are produced manually, some digitally, and some are composites: thematic drawings establish the topics for a project, a cosmology of ideas, frequently non-scaled and non-hierarchical; strategic plots plot things over and through time, often comprised of figures, text, diagrams, notations, and indexes; aspectival drawings establish the critical figurative attributes, or aspects of architecture without synthetic resolution; and cryptic drawings visualise the genetic, characteristics of a spatial proposition. The development of each of these drawing types was designed to work most appropriately on particular ideas in different phases of a project. All towards becoming an agile cultural agent, acting variably in different situations.

Gilles Retsin and Barry Wark

WHATSAPP CHAT: END-TO-END UNENCRYPTED

The following is an extract from a conversation over WhatsApp, across time zones, over a few days. In many ways, it is a snapshot of an ongoing debate between two colleagues and friends with many overlaps and a few differences.

GR So, tell me, what do you find truly exciting in architecture today?

BW I am generally excited by architecture that attempts to meet some of the challenges of our contemporary world while not wholly throwing computational design tools out of the window, which is a worrying trend. Specifically, I am excited by the return of structural stone and its ability to be both an ecological building material and beautiful. Also, those leveraging AI in a tool-building capacity, not just these exhausting text-to-image visualisations.

GR OK — I get that, though my question would be: where do you see the scope for computational tools and AI concerning, for example, structural stone? Architects such as Amin Taha have been pushing stone back on the agenda, but they do beautiful stone projects without AI or computational tools. It's just nice grids, which get a lot of quality from the materiality of the stone. There is a strand of work based on materiality that is now very in vogue (Anne Holtrop, Antón García Abril, Amin Taha). Rather than 3D-printing sand, they just extract a rock.

BW I love all that stuff but I'm curious whether stone can become more than a column or vertical structural element. Maybe right now, it feels like it's trending towards a sort of raw classicism. These design tools allow us to integrate more information and intelligence as we design beyond a grid. This could be environmental, structural, spatial, etc., but I think it will allow us to create something else, something more novel in its assembly and resulting form and aesthetics.

GR An AI that can assemble a building from a series of found objects (rocks, stones). We did that a few years ago with our Bartlett students as well.

BW One thing I'm interested in discussing regarding materials is that in many of your projects, you tend to use one material to do all the work. So, working with parts, a wall is a column, and a floor is a floor — all in one material. Why is that, and would you ever be interested in multi-material assemblies?

GR It's not just me; a major strategy in architecture is to reduce the number of materials used. If we look to the past, we also see these kind of very reduced material assemblies: a gothic cathedral using stone for almost everything, for example. Complex multi-material assemblies are a product of late-modernist over-optimisation, hyper-specialisation, and fragmentation of supply chains. Every material has an industrial supplier: Kingspan, Saint-Gobain, Wienerberger etc. Every material becomes a part with a specific function. All of these materials and suppliers then require a lot of architectural detailing and blood, sweat, and tears to be combined into a nice building. And if there is very little money for architecture, we tend to see buildings that then express their commodified parts: buildings that look like cheap cladding or cheap components, etc. I think the potential of the digital is to really reset this kind of environmentally unfriendly, complicated, and fragmented way of working and instead go for simple, blunt assemblies with just a few materials or parts, locally sourced. It works from an aesthetic and experiential perspective and makes sense from the point of view of production, the environment, automation, etc. It could also power an architecture that is easier to do in large amounts, easier to coordinate, easier to design, and get something nice out of it. I am personally interested in exploring this attitude but across a few materials: timber and stone, for example, or timber and brick. It really doesn't need to be just one material from an ideological point of view.

BW I'm on board with that, especially regarding the environmental aspect. In my work, I'm thinking about the potential multiple lives of buildings, their use and reuse, and what happens to elements when they have reached the point of failure through weathering. If they are too complex, they are hard to recycle or reformulate. But to the original question, I don't think it's unreasonable to say walls in stone and the spans in timber.

GR Absolutely. There is a nice case to make stone or brick structures that have a long lifespan and then have timber operate in shorter cycles, being more adaptive, etc. Ultimately these are very old ideas, and that's maybe something interesting to talk about. I've always positioned the thesis that the digital and automation return architecture to a more primordial core. It's an undoing of modernist late-capitalist industrial systems and replacing them with a mode of making closer to pre-modern times but powered by tech. I would say this is a very different attitude to the future than we see in the work of the early digital, which dwelt more on glossy, immaterial aesthetics and spaces. Your work is also associated with 'the ancient'. Do you want to talk a bit about how that came to be or what it means?

BW I think this temporal aspect that you refer to of different parts on a site for various periods is precisely what my work is exploring right now. Regarding 'ancientness', which is different from your preferred term of 'primitiveness' in that it always implies a temporal dimension. For me, 'ancient' is interesting for two reasons. First, it suggests a way of building that you alluded to above that is maybe crude and less focused on the structural gymnastics of early 'digital' work, which, in that way, shares notions of primitiveness. The second is about ecological aesthetics and weathering. We are more willing to accept these effects on structures we perceive as older than contemporary. A bit too much to write in WhatsApp, but essential in this is rejecting flatness and instead celebrating texture, articulation, and, dare I say it, ornament. This is different from the trend I see in your work, which seems to be blunter and much less fussy.

GR I remember when I was at your reviews at Penn, there was a discussion about the more implicit political associations that inevitably come with the aesthetics of 'ancientness': a kind of dark, Ruskinian, moody structure of feeling. 'It's dark times in Europe; let's all sit inside with some mulled wine at the fireplace' kind of feeling. I contrasted it with the optimism of the Superdutch, who in the 1990s dreamt big, did flashy things, and exported their work all over the world with a kind of promise of happy optimism and the

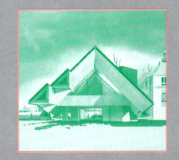

feeling that we could make and shape the world as we want it. They also spoke about society, economy, territorial scale thinking, etc. Do you sometimes feel that looking at material details, like a block of stone or brick, is a bit limiting? Do you relate to that kind of moody, dark feeling I described, or are you happier than that ;)?

BW I don't think you can easily distinguish these things; I can be happy or sad drinking mulled wine by a fire and the same with a sparkling lime drink on a beach (although I do agree both can affect us differently). Similarly, a soot-blackened gothic cathedral feels very different in the sun than in the rain. That sentiment you are touching upon is my earnest exploration of what the aesthetics of the environmental project in architecture could be beyond the sweetness of today's plant-filled facades. It's stuck in the bio-utopias of the mid- to late-twentieth century; the world and our understanding of the environment and ecology have changed since then. I feel awful and optimistic about the environment at the same time. Architecturally, this is where the parts come in; if we conceive buildings as open assemblies with different temporal presences, some could be older, 'ancient', and display deeper ecological enmeshment, whereas others could be more pristine and cleaner. It's both a ruin and new; it's never either/or. Regarding the brick comment, my work is obviously about more than a detail-level consideration. That said, I think it's essential to keep the human scale in mind when we design, especially if we are talking about architecture in large quantities, which can be lost due to the scale of what is being designed. You champion the Georgian terrace in your work. Those buildings have lots of details that people love (along with other things). So, are you up for some detail and intricacy? Or are you sadder than that ;)?

GR Actually, the success of the Georgian terrace is often attributed to the fact that it stripped back detail to just a few precise locations: lintels and entry porch. The rest is pretty abstract. That's why I find them so attractive as a model as well. It's just a play with the white fenestration in brick facades. That said, I agree that we should not be afraid of intricacy. My work comes out of intricacy, and I guess it's a continuous questioning of the meaning of intricacy. How much do we need and when? I am interested in understanding that. For example, if something works without a lot of intricacy, why do the intricacy? What I like about your work is that you are also very precise. There are more abstract parts without much detail and then precise interventions where you decide to add detail. Historically, this was also the way to go as detail ultimately in the past always meant some form of labour and energy.

BW Totally, but those small features make a world of difference; when we see the pastiche version of those houses built in London without those details, they feel a little sad. Maybe it doesn't mean labour as much now with digital fabrication tools, but it still means money, and projects have budgets, so you need to pick and choose your spots. But I will summarise that as a 'yes' from you.

GR With your ecological and aesthetic arguments, I know it's all earnest, but I am just curious what you think of my question about optimism. It's something I question a lot. I feel Europe has been bogged down by a degrowth mentality, where we believe the future is over, it's no longer our time, etc. Our future is building straw huts, and forming little communities, etc. In the meantime, the Saudis are building entirely new cities. So, in that sense, I always make this connection between this affinity for the primitive/ancient (which is shared) and that kind of epochal pessimism.

BW I understand the optimism question, which resonates with me too. I feel like it's a vital role for architects to give vision to the future with some substance (or else it can become sci-fi). We need balance; yes, we need to be optimistic, but it can't just be a blind utopia. That is what I detest about these urban visions that rely on covering the proposals in plants. They are full of optimistic sentiments, all shiny and new, with a return to the Garden of Eden just around the corner, but I'm never convinced. I don't see primitiveness or ancientness as synonymous with a 'good old days' mentality. I think if the work is leveraging technology to address contemporary social/cultural/political issues, then it is an avenue worth exploring for some of the reasons outlined before. What's interesting about the optimism question is that you've alluded to the scale of projects or the investigation (beyond building details). The question is, what agency can a singular building have in the world? In your opinion, how big do they or their ideas need to be to have meaningful agency? And how do you even define that?

GR For me, that's a critical question. I have always been interested in the design problem of how to design repetition. It's harder to design a building that repeats twenty times next to itself rather than a one-off. This is not to say that I don't enjoy one-offs, but that fascination for architecture that can repeat itself in exciting ways is what drives my work now with AUAR. It also underlies my work with GRA, but I am using singular cases more as methods to test repeating systems. Also, now that I am working on AUAR, it means that I am pivoting GRA more in the direction of the singular and the unexpected. They're both different modes of practice — a tech company for the many and an experimental architecture practice for the few. But yes, I think there is scope now in the world to try and do architecture in large quantities, a smart form of repetition rather than focusing on the iconic, unexpected one-off. That has had its time, and its impact/societal agency is limited. What the world is looking for now is approaches that can do something for people and for the planet. So, while I like to observe all the fantastic creative ideas that architects come up with today, I also wonder what these mean and if this is what we should be doing right now.

RESCUE LINES

Smout Allen

Rescue Lines proposes a world in which the forests of the United Kingdom, both ancient and modern, can be expanded, restored, and connected once again. Our project takes the form of a series of south-to-north ecological bridges — linear super-landscapes — along which displaced or endangered species can safely travel, and threatened human economies can thrive.

At the heart of Rescue Lines, elaborate forest 'proving grounds' serve to host new prototype landscapes. Inside these experimental facilities, species hardened against climate change will be both cultivated and preserved, forming tactical landscape 'starter packs', ready for planting elsewhere. Within these proving grounds, resident stewards will also monitor speculative plant-measurement labs: whole-tree temperature chambers, soil-acid gauges, canopy-enrichment nets, and deep-ground rhizotrons where members of the public can watch in real time as roots expand through designer soil.

"Once again I see,

These hedgerows,

hardy hedgerows,

Little lines of

sportive wood run wild."

William Wordsworth

Housing is constructed around shared, circular plots. Each home also serves as a valve, rather than a barrier, for the surrounding landscape: the structures are pierced with voids, tunnels, and hollows allowing vegetation and wildlife to pass through. This connects each hedge/house to the existing matrix of hedgerows and holloways throughout the United Kingdom.

Here, caretakers and their families wander along risen walkways and maintenance walls, exploring their gardens and woods. Stewards for the orchards live on-site in homes shaded by the very trees they study, pollarding and pruning branches as if tending their own private rooms.

Worms, birds, moulds, and other species also live here, eager to follow the northward expansion of our 'rescue lines', tracking the warming gradients of the planet's collective future. Even the internal sounds of this new, climate-adapted ecology can be checked daily inside recording studios staffed by acousticians trained to hear the subtlest notes of landscape change.

Rescue Lines explores the future of green infrastructure through the lives of those who engage with it. Our project connects ecological zones and economic territories at the same time, suggesting that longitudinal lines of connection, bridging forests across the United Kingdom as a model for sites elsewhere, can help us all prepare — hectare by hectare — for a climate-changed world.

Mark West

These Drawings

I can't say that these drawings are 'architectural' in the sense that they represent or describe buildings to be built. Obviously they are not. Imagine instead shuffling forwards in the dark, hands and fingers stretched out ahead, waiting to receive what they will touch.

After losing faith in received modes of architectural representation (think mechanically formed lines), the search was on for a proper realism, one that might more accurately describe the true nature of the physical world we live in now. The convincing illusion that the world is composed of solid 3-D objects ordered in empty 3-D space is a hard one to shake. There is a long-established inventory of tools that help build and confirm this illusion. Be careful which ones you pick up.

You might say these drawings are preparations — my offerings of a more realistic appraisal of present conditions. And what have the fingers found? A world full of colour. A scalar density that never gives up. The dry and the wet; the hard and the soft; the cool and the warm; attraction and repulsion … all the old alchemical opposites abide with their pleasures and irritations. Bodies and machines, once clearly distinct, grow towards compresence.

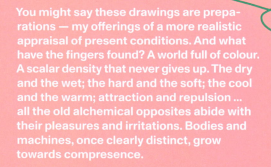

Look closely and it's obvious that the plenum is always packed. There is no empty space. There are no empty sites. And there are certainly no lines between things. All our actions only displace one volume of atoms with another. Here you might brush up against your robot assistant, robot slave, robot boss, robot mother, robot father. All these things come from the earth, from the air. Artificial hearts; drone shots and sonar signals, solar flares and clouds of dust, lichens on polystyrene, semiconductors in the wet market … boundaries form and dissolve through knots and entanglements. The full inventory and its recombinations endlessly reappear in manifold forms of ancient aversions and new and alluring beauties.

And a fire is always burning somewhere to power the thing forwards. I thought we made solid things, but they turned out to be temporal gatherings. I thought they were just made of material, but found out they were always only energy — or what passes for it. Our constructions are a separation of energised matter holding entropy at bay by constant inputs of energy, maintenance schedules, and the occasional gut renovation. Long supply chains leave tread-marks and inevitable footprints, and the whole edifice vibrates with a continuous flow of electrons, unexpectedly generating massive clouds of data.

Your perceptions may vary. The small, printed versions of these images now in your hands, I am sorry to say, produce a weaker sauce than the meal served up in the actual drawing. My aspirations towards realism hope for the kind of scalar density offered by the microscope and the telescope; a continuous and never-ending unspooling of form and re-formation. What looked like an object is revealed as a gathering. What looked like a gathering is revealed as an object. Or so it appears.

BACK TO THE FUTURE

One of the most important elements of *Archigram's* work was the concept of responsive environments. In the 1960s, we were limited by the lack of technological tools to develop architecture that could interact dynamically with its occupants. Now, we have the tools, but the enthusiasm and drive to use them are missing. It's a curious change from a time when the possibilities excited many, despite the technological limitations.

Today, none of our built environments, from individual dwellings to entire cities, are truly responsive. This is a significant missed opportunity. For instance, in my original drawing of the Computer City, I included all the electronic components necessary to create a responsive environment. London Transport, for example, has the capability to monitor the exact number of passengers in the Underground system at any time. However, this information is not used to improve the operations on the ground.

In the late 1960s and early 1970s, there were architectural practices that engaged in real, ground-breaking work on responsive environments. It wasn't merely theoretical. Legislation played a role back then. Today, there's no legislation driving the development of responsive architecture, despite extensive experience in areas such as housing and city management.

Looking to the future, I envision an environment where architecture responds dynamically to the changing needs of its occupants. This is a large-scale problem that requires more than just individual architects theorising; it demands an industry-wide capability to respond. In the 1960s and '70s, system building was a subject of discussion, but now it's non-existent. Politicians repeatedly aim for high housing-production targets without addressing the practical necessities required to achieve those goals.

To produce the required 300,000 domestic units annually, we need an integrated industry that spans from theory to construction. This is not just about creating new products but about fostering a cultural shift. We must start by addressing the core problems, such as the availability of materials and land. Comprehensive planning is needed, but there is a lack of responsibility in current political agendas.

If we are to achieve such ambitious goals, we need both political and practical strategies. In the 1960s, various industries, including the aircraft industry, were heavily involved in such forward-thinking projects. Today, we need similar industrial engagement.

We must move from critique to proposition, linking past ideas from *Archigram* to future perspectives. By revisiting and building upon the innovative proposals of the 1960s, we can make actionable steps towards a future where responsive architecture is a reality.

Dennis Crompton

I'VE GOT AN IDEA

Todd Gannon

I gather a sampling of architecture books from my library, fling them open across the desk, and pry my pre-teen offspring from their screens for an assessment. 'Pick one,' I say.

The boy slaps a centrefold alive with crane-capped frames, telescoping tubes, curious accretions of geodesic domes, and miles of tubular conduits.

The girl hesitates: 'This would be all colourful in real life, right?'

'Of course.'

She slaps the same page and skips away.

*

A group of middle-aged professionals make small talk at a cocktail party. 'I always wanted to be an architect …' claim a doctor, a lawyer, an accountant.

*

A couple of talented young architects chat in their studio. They're bored with their day jobs and pining for the excitement that attracted them to architecture school a few years before. 'I've got an idea.' One of them ventures.

*

Sixty years ago, sixteen years ago, six minutes ago, talented young architects, would-be architects, future architects are tickled by the promise of seductive images and begin to imagine alternative futures.

'Hey David, isn't this great?'

'Yes Peter,

but look at this.'

In one of those instances, the young architects commandeer the office mimeograph to help broadcast their affection for a certain kind of exuberant form-making.

'A new generation of architecture must arise', they implore. Within a few years, it did.

The first nine and a half issues of *Archigram* tell the story of that generation. Page after exuberant page, they trace those young architects' wide-ranging enthusiasm — sometimes prescient, sometimes naïve, always provocative, never dull — and their infectious desire for something different, something better that within a few short years circled the globe.

Plug in!

Switch on!

Ready? Zooooooom!

Even now, fifty years since that last half-issue, Peter and David, Dennis, and Spider, and the rest that remain of the *Archigram* generation, still sparkle with the optimism of their youth. They still draw 'for the sheer hell of doing it', as another Peter famously put it, and this tenth issue of their famous little magazine still exudes that optimistic joie de travailler that both complements and transcends the responsibilities of professional competence and the machinations of disciplinary ambition. Staking a claim in the heart of the twenty-first-century future those young architects once imagined with wide-eyed enthusiasm, this issue of *Archigram*, like each issue before, pins its hope on a new generation, the next generation, the draw-first-and-ask-questions-later generation that establishes the terms — and sets the tone — for the future of the field.

'Hey Spider, isn't this great?'

'Yes Dennis, but look at this!'

Mark West

Perry Kulper

Neil Denari

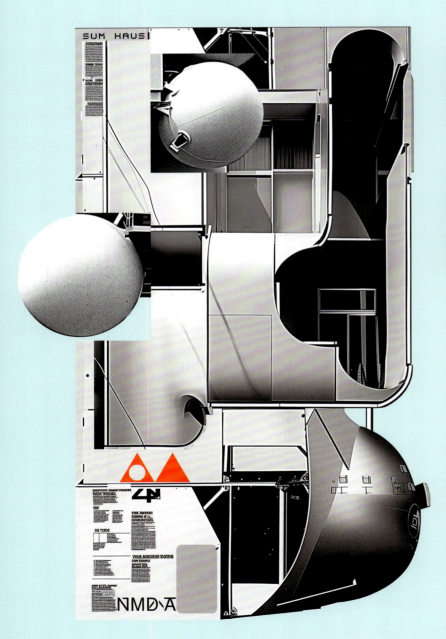
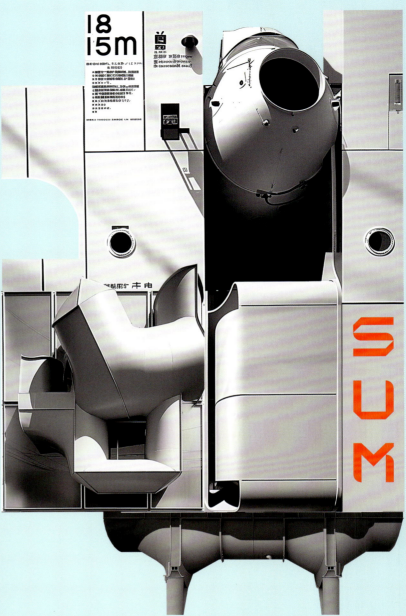

Nasrine Seraji

THOUGHTS
WORDS
DRAWINGS

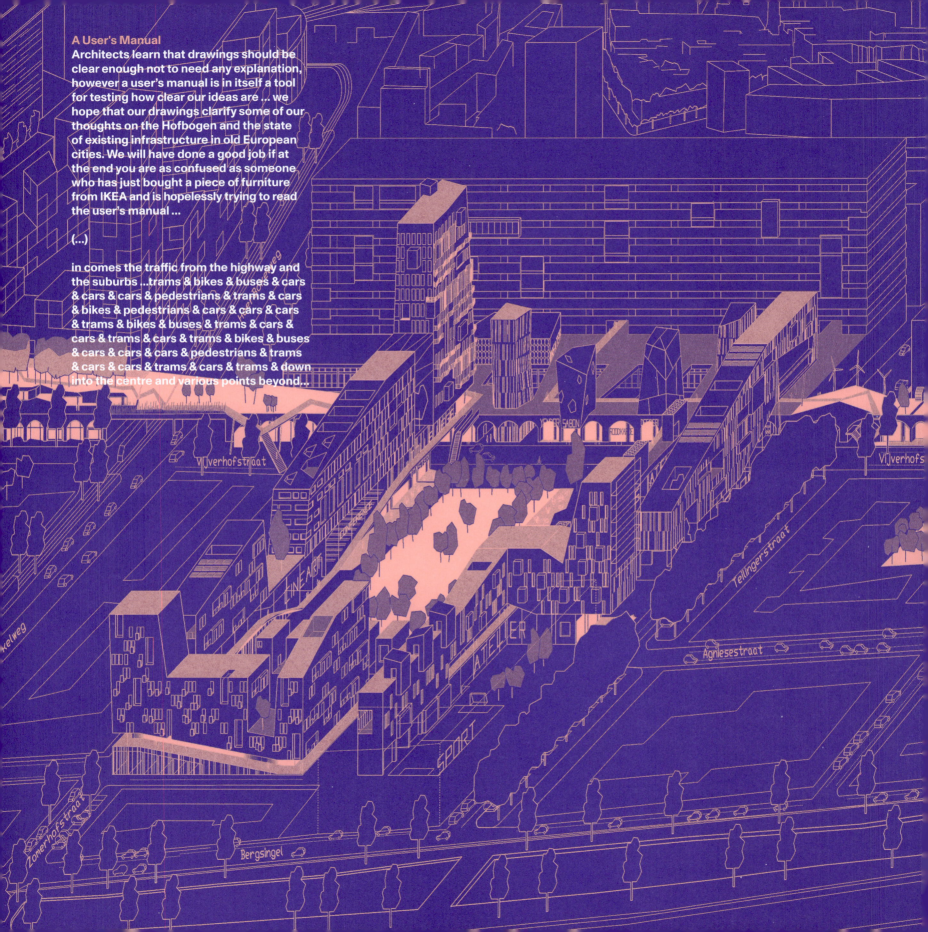

A User's Manual
Architects learn that drawings should be clear enough not to need any explanation, however a user's manual is in itself a tool for testing how clear our ideas are ... we hope that our drawings clarify some of our thoughts on the Hofbogen and the state of existing infrastructure in old European cities. We will have done a good job if at the end you are as confused as someone who has just bought a piece of furniture from IKEA and is hopelessly trying to read the user's manual ...

(...)

in comes the traffic from the highway and the suburbs ...trams & bikes & buses & cars & cars & cars & pedestrians & trams & cars & bikes & pedestrians & cars & cars & cars & trams & bikes & buses & trams & cars & cars & trams & cars & trams & bikes & buses & cars & cars & cars & pedestrians & trams & cars & cars & trams & cars & trams & down into the centre and various points beyond...

CITY ON Hitoshi Abe THE MOVE

Technological advances and changes in labour practices during the modern period caused a spatial, programmatic, and ideological divide, separating places of moving, working, and domestic activity. This strict division became a key concept of modernism fundamental to shaping the static roles of architecture and urban design. While this paradigm creates the cities we live in today, recently these three environments have begun to blend again, and places hitherto defined by a single fixed role are becoming more fluid.

This convergence has been triggered by the recent fusion of the workplace and domestic place, which began around 2000, with the development of communication technology. Since then, society has gradually welcomed co-working and co-living scenarios, which have begun to attract a niche cross-section of specific industries and people. The 2020 pandemic accelerated the convergence of work and living spaces by forcing companies to relinquish their traditional office typologies and allow people to work remotely. In this post-pandemic world, companies and employees are questioning the traditional work-life relationship.

Various new industries are emerging that focus on integrated work-life environments, and new forms of communities and typologies. Furthermore, changes in mobility, such as the diversification of mobility through ridesharing services such as Uber and Bird, the diversification of the concept of ownership triggered by the shared economy, such as that of Airbnb, and the ability for activities during transit triggered by the development of autonomous driving pursued by various car companies, are accelerating this tendency. These changes have shifted the concept of place from its traditionally fixed role as a destination into one in which its roles are more fluid. Sixty years after Walking City, the city has finally begun to move.

INFRASTRUCTURE AS MATTER OF DESIGN

Sille Pihlak

Infrastructure design plays a crucial role in shaping both rural and urban landscapes, yet it often consists of unremarkable engineered elements lacking in architectural distinction. However, there lies untapped potential in these structures to become focal points of identity and placemaking. For instance, power transmission lines, typically mundane and uniform, possess the capacity to be transformed into emblematic symbols within our environment.

As the world is in transition towards fossil-free energy sources, the prominence of power production and transmission infrastructure is bound to increase. No longer can infrastructure be relegated to the background; it demands attention and consideration. To echo the sentiments of Bruno Latour, the infrastructure is something that can't be hidden away and has shifted from being taken for granted to being a matter of significant concern. In the light of this, we must reimagine these seemingly utilitarian structures as artistic landmarks, blending structural efficiency with contextual relevance.

By infusing design-led elements into their construction, we can elevate them from mere functional entities to integral components of our cultural and visual landscapes. Consequently, highways and other spaces dominated by monotonous vistas can be enlivened by the addition of strategically placed, aesthetically pleasing structures that celebrate their surroundings while serving their practical purposes. Infrastructure is a matter of design.

Architects solve problems. We analyse difficulties, grasp potential, and use our imagination to transform them. As problem solvers, there is no better architectural mentor than nature's exemplars. Nature abounds with evolving systems and organisms that respond effectively to crisis, scarcity, and opportunity.

Technology, currently undergoing dramatic redefinition, should also be learning from and connecting to nature. It is important to embed technology with human intuition and with nature's vast quarry of intelligence. Fusing digital and empirical tools will catalyse a new way of thinking, doing, and constructing, creating a technology that is a super-symbiosis of nature and human nature.

Tonkin Liu

SHELL LACE

STRUCTURE

Shell Lace Structure was invented by Tonkin Liu in 2009 and developed in collaboration with engineers at Arup. The single-surface structural technique combines mollusc shells' structural principle with the ancient tailoring craft, using contemporary digital design and fabrication tools, to make super-strong, super-lightweight structures requiring minimal materials.

The Tower of Light is a 40-metre-tall single-surface structure in Manchester's Civic Quarter that supports and encloses the flues of the low-carbon energy centre. The undulating surface is constructed from 6mm-thick laser-cut steel sheets whose stiff welded form locks in strength. The tower heralds Manchester's low-carbon future and communicates Manchester Council's aim 'to engage all individuals in a process of cultural change'.

AN OASIS OF LIVING CELLS

This is an oasis project in the middle of the modern city — a school currently in the design phase in the UAE. The school is a retrofit in a listed modern building, which still appears futuristic half a century after its construction.

The plan reflects an entirely new approach to education. The planning resembles the composition inside a living cell. There are no hard boundaries, and there are shared spaces between classrooms. As there are many elements with specific functions, each room is floating as an autonomous cell yet interconnected with the space like cytoplasm. Education is evolving from teaching to learning. While teaching is the process to convey knowledge from a teacher to students, learning is a much more individual activity to gain wisdom to survive in the real world. Unlike traditional linear school planning, the classrooms are randomly placed to enable multidisciplinary relationships.

The shape of the existing shell allows traditional natural ventilation to be utilised to extract warm air. The project will include an oasis-like landscape project surrounding the building. The perimeter will be edged with shallow waterworks. The landscape acts as a sponge to catch rainwater, which will provide evaporative cooling.

The building is the representation of the future of education and also self-sufficient microclimate.

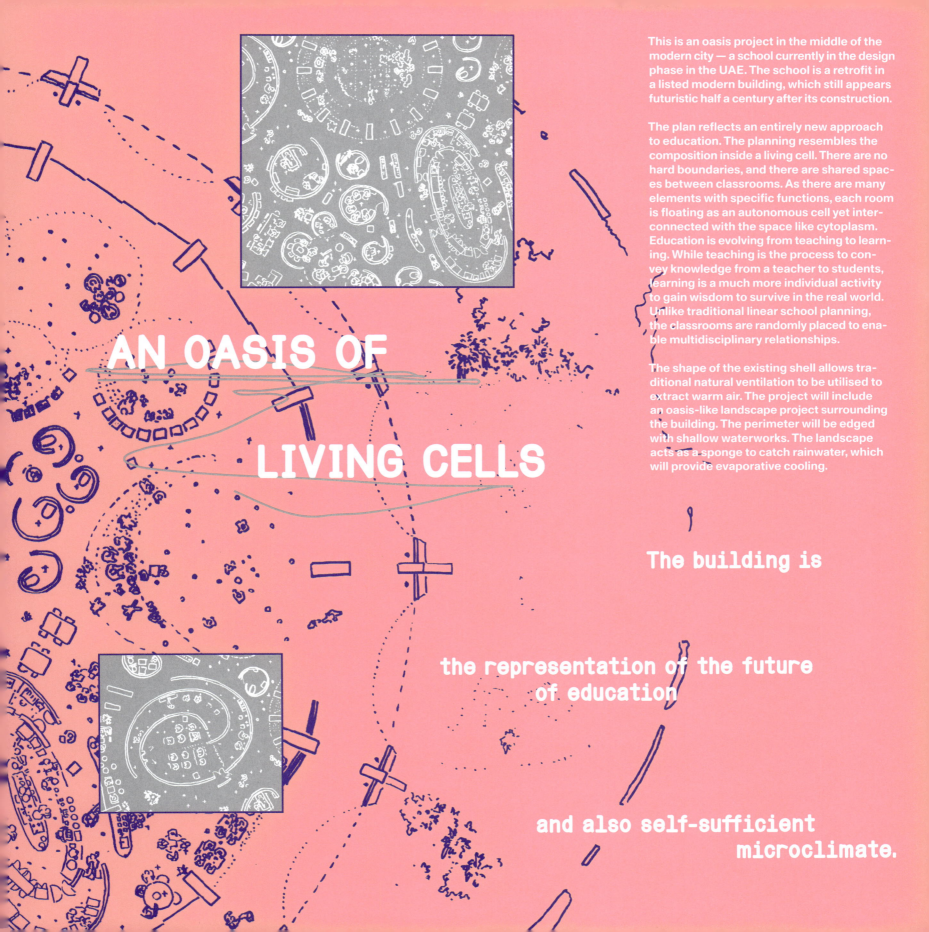

BUDAPEST MUSEUM

This project introduces a new possibility of how the art and the pleasure of being in the park can interact, how art could and should be presented in dialogue with architecture and culture at large, and the museum not be just a vessel, but an agent of provocation towards art and its different forms of production. The museum takes you inside in a friendly manner, extending the city and the park into its interior, the museum elevates itself to allow the park and city to continue their dialogue.

The Visionary
The visionary as an imagining being is blind.

Anarchitecture
The architectural narrative, even before its design, is generated by the elaboration of any trace (shadows) other than the architecture itself. But it uses an entire city to construct it. The city as anarchitecture is re-imagined from its inner vestiges and myths.

Hybrids
Animal and wild nature [Leonardo da Vinci] as architectural genome constitute an intermediate space between architecture and nature (meta-n ature).

Exterior / Interior, Content / Container, Ancient / Contemporary, Past / Future, Utopian / Dystopian are [mental and physical] thresholds and thus the basis for the creation of imprecise, transparent, and constantly changing spaces.

Artificial Intelligence
Theatrum Mundi of artificial intelligence.

What the AI at its best, when cleverly prompted, makes up is a myth, an intimation of a world that have might existed [...] that might exist some day in the future [...] or may already exist, in the images, forms, evocations, and spaces anarchitects are recognising as much as producing. It's up to us to recognise them, to recite them, to make them our own, and use them to make a world that will be open to all.
[Aaron Betsky (2024), *The Monster Leviathan*, MIT Press, p.417]

THEATRUM MUNDI

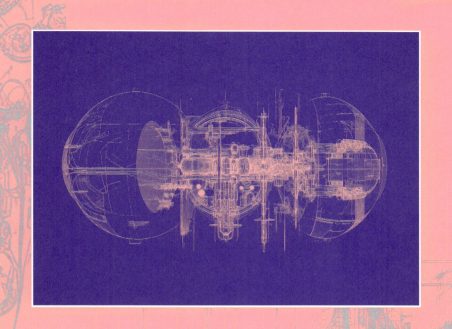

Cesare Battelli

Helen + Hard

REINHABITING THE CITY

Could Freya Matthews' panpsychic mindset, described as 'reinhabiting reality', help us re-imagine, reinvent, and reinvigorate our cities as the most authentic form of green living?

As she articulates: 'We have to re-enter a local modality of world, where we become interfused with place again, through a thorough attentiveness to the given it invites us to engage communicatively with … by entering into the fabric of the place we can slip beneath the skin of the world and the world is starting to respond to us …'

With this reciprocal enchantment, we can embark on a journey to reinhabit our cities through bold and imaginative dialogues — transforming, repurposing, interweaving, and revitalising. This involves converting grey into green, concrete into timber, and vacant office buildings into versatile spaces for diverse age groups, fostering care and collaboration. We envision apartment blocks transformed into vibrant communities with lush communal areas and rooftop gardens, while reclaiming privatised ground floors and roads to create verdant gardens and corridors that connect seamlessly with the natural landscape.

formalhaut is a group of architects / artists that for forty years has worked at the interface between art and architecture. The name is inspired by the cosmic name *fomalhaut*, a fixed star near the Sculptor constellation. We are intrigued and inspired by the source of Presence in the void.

Space and Presence
While ostensibly immaterial, there is also Presence in space that is vibrant and auratic, and we enjoy the creative potential. We create space and we create boundaries, but from where exactly does the Presence of our space emanate? Are the physical boundaries the agent, or does the Presence of space come from its void?

formalhaut
PRESENCE IN THE VOID

formaloskop

About the vastness of space
Our construct is defined by the place, by the memory of the dynamic function, our interest being the consequence on the universal void.

About the boundaries of the void
Small featherlight homes, easy to handle, transportable. Soft, clever construction offering temporary shelter, somewhere between building and clothing.

Our Medium, a component of travel, of transience, of the nomadic; high-tech equipment for adventurers with a pioneering mind to explore spaces in yet-unexplored territories.

Our Message, one of absence, dislodgement, migration, and rootlessness; a necessity for bare existence, a reminder of the social void, of a loss of permanence and security.

Our Construct, a temporary place in time, stability in the momentary collective. We prescribe the holistic Presence of the Archimedean Void, where the Solid is unattainable.

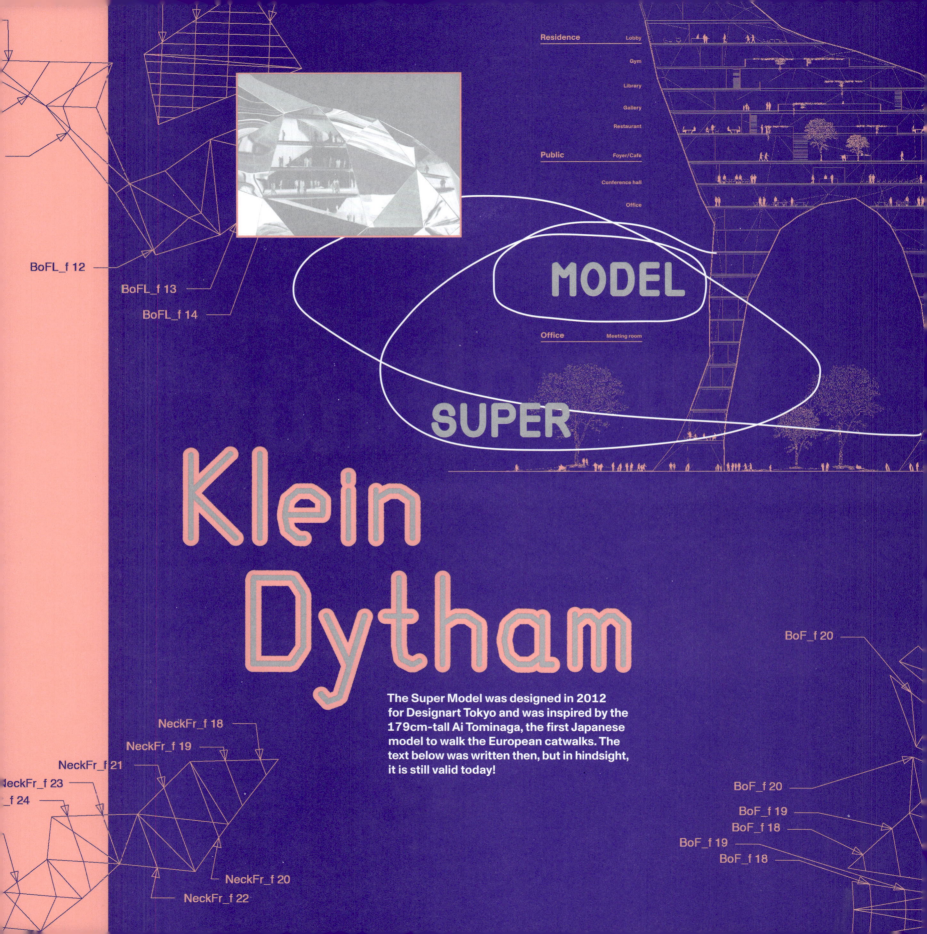

Klein Dytham

The Super Model was designed in 2012 for Designart Tokyo and was inspired by the 179cm-tall Ai Tominaga, the first Japanese model to walk the European catwalks. The text below was written then, but in hindsight, it is still valid today!

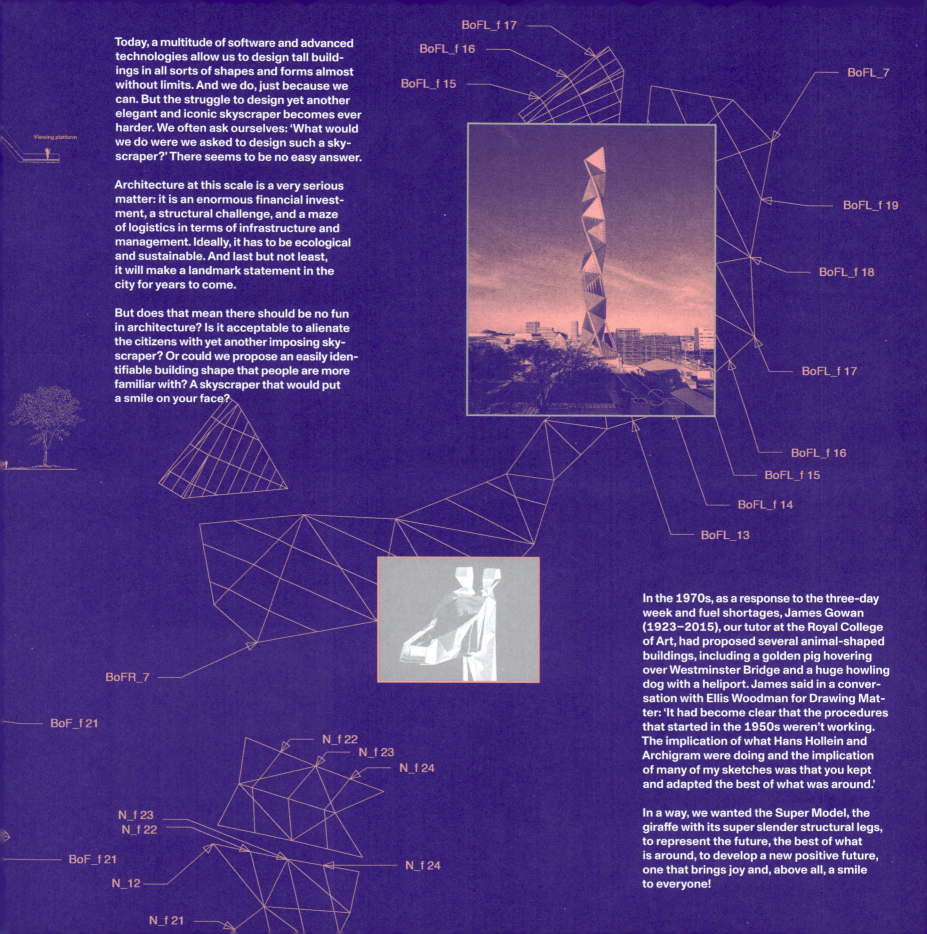

Today, a multitude of software and advanced technologies allow us to design tall buildings in all sorts of shapes and forms almost without limits. And we do, just because we can. But the struggle to design yet another elegant and iconic skyscraper becomes ever harder. We often ask ourselves: 'What would we do were we asked to design such a skyscraper?' There seems to be no easy answer.

Architecture at this scale is a very serious matter: it is an enormous financial investment, a structural challenge, and a maze of logistics in terms of infrastructure and management. Ideally, it has to be ecological and sustainable. And last but not least, it will make a landmark statement in the city for years to come.

But does that mean there should be no fun in architecture? Is it acceptable to alienate the citizens with yet another imposing skyscraper? Or could we propose an easily identifiable building shape that people are more familiar with? A skyscraper that would put a smile on your face?

In the 1970s, as a response to the three-day week and fuel shortages, James Gowan (1923–2015), our tutor at the Royal College of Art, had proposed several animal-shaped buildings, including a golden pig hovering over Westminster Bridge and a huge howling dog with a heliport. James said in a conversation with Ellis Woodman for Drawing Matter: 'It had become clear that the procedures that started in the 1950s weren't working. The implication of what Hans Hollein and Archigram were doing and the implication of many of my sketches was that you kept and adapted the best of what was around.'

In a way, we wanted the Super Model, the giraffe with its super slender structural legs, to represent the future, the best of what is around, to develop a new positive future, one that brings joy and, above all, a smile to everyone!

Takayuki Taki Suzuki

WRITE NOVELS AS AN ARCHITECT

'Write novels as an architect!' I read a message like that disseminated by Archigram when I was an architecture student in Japan, although I might be paraphrasing it. So I did precisely that and won the Gunzo Literature Award with my first novel *Portrait in Numbers*. We did not have the word 'parametric' for architecture at that time, but the novel already had a kind of parametric structure. I used the *'numbers'* as parameters, exactly what it means.

Now I believe we can design a novel with generative stories. The author and reader will both be able to modify the novel by changing the parameters to synchronise it with their own lives. I show the simplified method in Parametric Novel Diagram. It is for the new field of expression, an absolutely authentic literature or architecture.

Architecture appears as a 'synchroniser' in this diagram, like A Girl in Wuhan. In a narrow definition, architecture means synchroniser. However, the whole diagram can be called architecture if it includes urban design, interior design, historical research, and more.

A Girl in Wuhan appeared when I surveyed the old residential area in Wuhan, China. All things that once happened, are happening, and will happen, became visible with the girl. Everything real and illusory emerged from the alleys. The future began to loom larger than life.

Today, many architects say 'sustainability is our priority' or 'digital technology is the future'. A Girl in Wuhan shows the new relationship between these two issues. Essential sustainability exists only in stories in the city. The stories can be transformed by Parametric Novel Diagram to fit our lives. A Girl in Wuhan is there in the flesh, and also exists in the digital imagination. Borders between real and digital cities are vanishing.

Even after the Covid-19 situation showed us how digital and information technology can change the transport and planning of existing cities, some architects still believe in the necessity of freeways and functional zoning in the city. Actually, we can now have any function such as office, school, or entertainment, online in any space, therefore, both city and architecture are collective and temporal micro-functions in the same manner. Just Synchroniser in a city is architecture.

Synchroniser would also work as the origins of the next stories by showing strength, strangeness, or sometimes a crack in the reality of the city. But wait a minute … I can hear the whisper of A Girl in Wuhan. "What is there in the crack? Well, it's what I am still thinking. Maybe this is the next message to me, or you.

Gilles Retsin

ARCHITECTURE IN LARGE QUANTITIES

Working with AUAR/ABB Robotics

For a decade, the architectural ecosystem in London, between the Architectural Association and the Bartlett School of Architecture, was animated by lively debate around the interplay of architecture and technology. These discussions kicked off some time post-2008, marked by the global financial crisis, the sudden emergence of social network tech, and the unstoppable growth of Amazon. The time of the optimistic, glossy, fluid shapes and spaces that had sparked architecture enthusiasm since the early 1990s was starting to fade. The financial crisis had changed the vibe. Architecture biennales, educational platforms, and other institutions purged their programmes of all-too-outspoken techno-optimism.

A new generation emerged, with a keen interest in issues such as the climate emergency and the housing crisis, issues of labour, new modes of practice. Many rejected technology, and instead advocated forms of craft or small-scale community action, broadly inspired by anti-capitalist agendas. Suddenly, outspoken design was deemed slightly immoral. By 2020, one would often hear the argument that we should just stop building to save the planet.

Yet, within this generational shift, a contrarian faction emerged, with a very different position — albeit one that was far less popular. They proposed a different route for architecture: what if we used the power of automation to address these large issues of climate, housing, and labour? Automation, they argued, could become a framework to develop a new architectural paradigm. By removing the factor of labour from the equation, suddenly things that had seemed impossible before became possible.

We could build architecture that can be both sustainable, affordable, and unapologetically design driven. Beauty, algorithmically generated and build by robots, is free. We could break the polluting, wasteful, global supply chains and use locally sourced materials such as timber and stone. The labour to process these could be at marginal cost. Moreover, confronting the Promethean scale of the problem of climate and housing, automation could help deliver both speed and impact. Rather than virtue-signalling good intentions with small-scale laborious building processes, an automated architecture could actually address the millions of sustainable homes that the world so urgently needs.

The thinking of this contrarian faction comes out of a long history of architects engaging with computation and machines, tracing all the way back from the modernist framework of mechanisation, to the structuralists, and then via Cedric Price, and Archigram, to John Frazer and Achim Menges, among many other figures that created the unique architectural ecosystem in London.

It's in this context that Automated Architecture (AUAR) was born, a technology startup with a vision to make sustainable housing universally accessible. AUAR was founded in 2019, by Mollie Claypool and myself, after a decade of experimental research and practice, deeply influenced by that specific long history of computational design that animated the discussions in London over the past decades. ABB, as a global leader in electrification and automation technology, is one of AUAR's investors, and one of its earliest strategic partners.

This partnership also finds its roots somewhere in the London architectural circuit. In 2019, at the Tallinn Architecture Biennale, which ran under the title of 'Beauty Matters', Yael Reisner introduced us to Katrin Förster, Global Key Account Manager for Architects at ABB. Via Katrin, the connection to ABB Robotics UK was made, which led its CEO at the time, Nigel Platt, and its current CEO, Dermot Lynch, to visit a 1:1 housing prototype we had built in partnership with Hackney Council, in London. They immediately realised that they were looking at something quite different from the usual approaches to construction automation, and offered AUAR the use of a robot at their facilities in Milton Keynes.

From there, we managed to build and prototype our first demonstrators and gain momentum. Beginning 2024, ABB Robotics & Automation Ventures decided to join an investment round in AUAR, cementing the partnership. AUAR and ABB together have the profound ambition to revolutionise construction, and in doing so, revolutionise the way we live. We share a vision that automation can enable sustainable, affordable, and beautiful architecture on a large scale. AUAR's ambitious mission is to reshape the whole process of design and manufacturing of housing, enabling the existing industry with a technology stack of software and robotics.

Design is at the core of what AUAR does. A distributed network of architects works with our technology to develop housing typologies which can then be mass-produced in endless variations across a network of robotic micro-factories. Architects add specificity and unexpected quality to the homes we produce — stretching the limits of what our building systems can do. AUAR revives an old ambition of architecture to not think about buildings as unique, never-to-be-repeated one-offs, but instead to think about an architecture in large quantities. The early modernists thought like this as well.

Mies's Barcelona Pavilion was meant to be mass-replicated into entire neighbourhoods, as was Le Corbusier's Villa Savoye. Of course, the mass housing projects devised by modernism turned out slightly different. But, after a pause of seventy years, we're back at a time that asks for an architecture in large amounts — if we want to stay relevant as a profession at least. The numbers are there: according to the United Nations we will need to deliver two billion new homes by 2050. In partnering with AUAR, ABB inscribes itself in a bold and radical architectural project coming out of a lineage of thinking that emerged somewhere in London, many decades ago, one that had a keen interest in the impact of technology on the very core of the profession. You'll find more of that in this volume of *Archigram*, more ideas, provocations, and radical experiments that will end up changing the way we build and live.

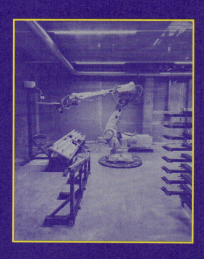

ARCHIGRAM TEN

First published in 2024
by Circa Press

©2024 Circa Press Limited,
Peter Cook and the contributors

CIRCA PRESS
50 Great Portland Street
London W1W 7ND
www.circa.press

Editor
PETER COOK

Co-editors
ELIN EYBORG LUND
DAVID JENKINS

Design
PG HOWLIN STUDIO

Proofreading
JULIA DAWSON

Typefaces
GAILE PRANCKUNAITE
ABC DINAMO

Printer
C&C OFFSET PRINTING CO., LTD

Archigram 10 has been realized with the generous support of ABB:

ABB is a global technology leader in electrification and automation, enabling a more sustainable and resource-efficient future. The company's solutions connect engineering know-how and software to optimize how things are manufactured, moved, powered and operated. Building on more than 140 years of excellence, ABB's 105,000 employees are committed to driving innovations that accelerate industrial transformation.

'The realisation of *Archigram 10* was a long-cherished wish by many. Having the chance to be part of the project and supporting Peter and his team means a lot to ABB. The future of architecture also depends on technologies where we are the champion and cooperation is key.'

KATRIN FÖRSTER
Global Key Account Manager at ABB

ISBN 978-1-911422-46-4

All rights reserved. No part of this publication may be reproduced or transmitted in any form or by any means, electronic or mechanical, including photocopy, recording or any other information storage and retrieval system, without prior permission in writing from the publisher.

Frozen Music

ABB IN ARCHITECTURE

Architecture is FROZEN MUSIC
ABB's video series spotlights outstanding architectural projects around the globe and the architects behind them.

'An Archigram tradition...

100
100 YEARS OF MCBs

MINIATURE **C**IRCUIT **B**REAKERS

A giant legacy of electrical safety

progressive sponsorship' PETER COOK